Ibrahim Aldasoqi, 978-1-62265-222-8 (online) 978-1-62265-223-5 (paper)

The World after Trump's Second Term Is the Nation's Most Dangerous Phase

Ibrahim Aldasoqi, Ph.D., MBA, MS

Publishing data: The World after Trump's Second Term Is the Nation's Most Dangerous Phase

English title: The World after Trump's Second Term Is the Nation's Most Dangerous Phase

Author's name in English: Ibrahim Aldasoqi, Ph.D., MBA, MS

ISBN information: 978-1-62265-222-8 (online) 978-1-62265-223-5 (paper)

Publishing time: March 2020.

Categories: Nonfiction > Politics

Editor / Designer: Bill Barton

Publishing location: New York, United States

Published by The International Institute for Science, Technology and Education (IISTE)

Contact of publisher: book@iiste.org

Printing facility: ColorWorks Limited.

```
9 781622 652228
```

Price: 19.99 USD / paper version

Ibrahim Aldasoqi,   978-1-62265-222-8 (online) 978-1-62265-223-5 (paper)

Author Bio

Ibrahim Aldasoqi, Ph.D., MBA, MS is an adjunct professor of Principle management at the University of Memphis and he was an online professor at the Arkansas State University. He is an outstanding academician with three Master's degrees in Business Administration, Political Sciences, and Hospitality and Resort Management and a Doctorate Degree in Political Sciences. He is currently enrolled in a DLS-Liberal Studies course at the Memphis University anticipating completion in 2020. Ibrahim was awarded the U.S. Department of State Certificate of Appreciation in 2013, and the Royal Court Certificate of Appreciation in the same year. Ibrahim has served as a hospitality administrator in the Royal Court of Jordan (Palace of the King), and supported President Barack Obama's and other international dignitaries procession in the Royal Court.

Ibrahim is a political science scholar and expert with over 10 years' experience in international relations, sales & revenue management, budget & sales strategy and international relations. He is a scholar with unending knowledge about the political landscape and its impact on national and global relations. He is passionate about public service, liberal democracy, foreign policy, government and America's relationship not only with its people but also with its leaders, other nations and international agencies.

Guided by this expertise, Ibrahim has authored a new book titled *'The World After Trump's Second Term is the Nation's Most Dangerous Phase'* that provides an irrefutable and authentic position on the state of the nation following President Donald Trump's Tenure. The book provides an expert position with indisputable facts on the negative toll that the Trump Presidency will reign on this country.

Above all these qualifications, Ibrahim is a citizen, a father and a son of this great nation.

Contents

Ibrahim Aldasoqi,   978-1-62265-222-8 (online) 978-1-62265-223-5 (paper)

Introduction

Americans are currently in an era of significant uncertainty. The previous conventions that shaped the political landscape have disappeared to be replaced by, well, Donald Trump and Trumpism. It is not clear what impact this political overhaul will have for America. Of course, making predictions about the future is hard, but a period did exist when political professors, pundits, and politicians could at least anticipate where they were headed as a country. America's foreign policy and relationships were secure, democracy was heavily protected, institutions were independent, and most importantly, the country was not led by a politically inexperienced president. There was optimism and dare I say confidence in the possibility of a future of liberal democracy. Today, instead, there is panic.

To quash this ever growing anxiety, it may be helpful to take a stand and perhaps try to map out what the future of America will look like in the next 4 to 10 years and in the long term. How will Trump's election, his ideologies, political approach, and actions affect America, its institutions, and its core political value? In other words, what is the future of America after Trump? This book presents a breakdown of the critical areas that have been affected by the Trump Presidency from the economy, democracy, constitution, Supreme Court, trade to the face of the political party. It is broken down into nine different chapters each highlighting Trump's effect on these issues and how this effect is very critical to the continued success and future of America as the greatest country on earth.

The book begins with a detailed discussion of what has been popularly dabbed Trumpism, a propagation of fear, hatred and threats thinly veiled as a president who is

1

unafraid to say what needs to be said. Trumpism put aside every political convention that gave even a semblance of diplomacy in the arena of public service and instead installed Trump as the only leader in the race willing to do what was necessary to save America. The reality is of course different because upon taking office, Trump's first term has been nothing short of a train wreck characterized by dishonesty, ignorance, misinformation, nepotism, narcissism and unending falsehoods. His effects cannot just be felt by those working with him, but even by the Republican Party with which he is affiliated, and almost every independent institution put in place to protect the rights of the American. There is not one entity that has been able to chain his errant behavior, because he has out rightly attacked the free media, assumed the commitments he made to his political party and blatantly ignored direct orders from Congress. The outcome of his election and first term really, is a country at the cusp of uncertainty not knowing whether it will collapse or come out strong, and a people so laden with fear it is concerning.

The discussion of Trump's perilous first term is then followed up by an examination of the possibility of Trump, despite his unmatched shortcomings as a president succeeding to earn a second term in office. The chapter assesses the reasons why Trump wants a second term from the big wall separating Mexico and the United States, his fixation on increasing the military budget, and his unexplained need to shrink the government among other factors. It also outlines the reasons why Trump is actually likely to succeed in reelection especially because throughout his presidency, Trump has been vetted time and again and still managed to survive. His impeachment trial especially, is thoroughly discussed detailing how the trial ensures that the country will experience no surprises

Ibrahim Aldasoqi,   978-1-62265-222-8 (online) 978-1-62265-223-5 (paper)

with Trump because it already knows Trump's track record and there are Americans who still believe that it is a positive track record.

Following the exploration of his current and possible future presidency, the book begins its scrutiny on Trump's effect on different institutions critical to the American foundation. Chapter three assesses whether the Supreme Court and the constitution will survive Trump if he does get a second term. It highlights the current grip that he has on the Supreme Court and how he has repeatedly attacked this independent institution to bend it to the shape that he desires. It also highlights his continued assault and disregard for the constitution. This is highlighted in the book by his nepotism and his disregard for the Emolument's clause and the consequential conflicts of interest that arise with his foreign businesses and his role as presidency. Are his foreign policy decisions as the presidency made to benefit his personal businesses and is he motivated by the need to protect the American people or his financial interest?

This then leads to a discussion of Trump's effect on the economy. Since he took office, Trump has made enemies of America's trade partners and alienated the country in trade agreements. The president's decision to withdraw from the Trans-Pacific Partnership (TPP), his approach to the NAFTA (Mexico and Canada) and KORUS (South Korea) renegotiations, his decision to block the appointment of the World Trade Organization (WTO) appellate body members, and the new tariffs put in place on aluminum and steel imply that Trump is no longer playing by the rules. What is most concerning is the trade war on tariffs that Trump begun with China. The chapter will place focus on how Trump took a confrontational approach with China, a country from which America relies heavily especially because majority of America's production takes place in China. It will highlight the impact of this trade war especially with sharp reductions in bilateral trade, higher prices for consumers and more struggles for farmers and manufactures who depend on China's production prowess.

Trump's unhinged approach to leadership raises questions about whether his leadership style will shape politics in future. Will the public lose trust in its political body after all the antics Trump has presented? Will the value of the vote remain? What about issues of unity and issues regarding civic membership. Most importantly, how will efforts to impeach him shape the political arena? Chapter 5 will focus on the future of America and how the political atmosphere will be if after all of his antics with false information, lack of diplomacy, or even attack on the media the public will stop supporting him or he is impeached. It also assesses the impact of a continued Republic win on the politics especially with regards to liberal democracy and issues such as equality, civic membership, universal healthcare, immigration, reproductive rights, and gun control. The issue is that the country will be relegated to a more conservative and traditionally obsolete form of leadership that does not go hand in hand with the trends and changes occurring today. The effects of Trump's leadership on the democracy are well highlighted in chapter 6 which highlights Trump's anti-democratic tendencies and how Trump's ideologies, decisions, and actions erode the very core of the American foundation, its democracy.

Chapter 7 and 8 highlight the irreversible effects that Trump's policies have had and will continue having on global issues including climate change and arms. Trump's stance on climate change and his subsequent policies will lead to irreversible global warming. For instance, his government worked to lower restrictions on methane emissions and to roll back climate change regulations a situation that is likely to have immense negative impacts on the climate in the long term. It does not do to have a president who does not believe in climate change but instead who focuses on nuclear weaponry. It is especially concerning that Trump's government has approved additional funding for spending in nuclear warfare in the guise of eliminating low-yield weapons in the U.S. In the same breath Trump has torn up long term nuclear arms treaties such as the Intermediate Range Nuclear Forces Treaty (INF). The problem is that actions such as these increase the risk of nuclear confrontation because the treaties that helped to prevent all nuclear war have been dismantled by Trump and because of him, America must exist in a highly unregulated and indisputably dangerous world where the threat of nuclear war looms.

Expanding on Trump's impact on global issues is his misguided foreign policy vision that is examined in chapter 9. This chapter will assess the impact of Trump's policies on America's relationship with Iran, Israel, Egypt, Turkey, Syria, Iraq and the Islamic State. It will also highlight the impact that Trump's trade agreements will have not just on America but on global markets. Trump has taken to coercion against America's partners. He has managed to increase the risk of nuclear war, and raised global doubts about the reliability and judgement of the U.S. The trade war with China, the NAFTA renegotiations, and the exit from the INF treaty are evidence of this. What these indicate is that America is currently headed by a president with poor impulse control and one who would risk war to get his way.

All in all, these chapters perfectly highlight exactly what Trump is not, a good president. They are a call for America to wake up and see that the future of America is doomed if at its helm sits Donald Trump.

Ibrahim Aldasoqi,   978-1-62265-222-8 (online) 978-1-62265-223-5 (paper)

The greatness of America lies not in being more enlightened than any other nation, but rather in her ability to repair her faults – Alexis de Toucqueville

"Donald Trump represents a threat both to the party and to the country. I believe he makes the world far more dangerous, I believe he puts America's economy in jeopardy. And his temperament is totally unsuited for the presidency" – Mitt Romney

Ibrahim Aldasoqi, 978-1-62265-222-8 (online) 978-1-62265-223-5 (paper)

Chapter One: Trump's First Term on Office

On November 8, 2016, a large portion of the country was shocked when Donald J. Trump was elected to be the 45th President of the United States. Many believed that Hillary Clinton who had won the popular vote, and significantly led almost all the pre-election polls would take the lead. It was probably among the saddest days in American electoral history and will be remembered as one that brought immense uncertainty to global politics. But who is Trump?

Currently the 45th president of the United States, Trump's resume defines him as a real estate mogul and a former reality TV star. Unlike his opponents, Trump had not held public office prior to his election, he had not been nurtured by a popular political party, he had not developed a group of political or policy advisers, and he had never spoken or thought systematically about the role and position of America in the world. In short, he was an 'outrageous political outsider' that no one, not even his campaign team, or other political observers expected to win.

But he did win, assisted by the backhanded transformation of the political process into an entertainment process 'Trumpism', blatant electoral fraud and foreign assistance. Thanks to Trump, America has had to endure inexperience, lies, tactlessness, and plain bigotry. This chapter highlights these key characteristics of the 45th President. It will outline how the concept of Trumpism began, how this has left a large stain on not only just national politics but also party politics and diplomacy, and how Trump's madness will leave a negative impact on the future of America's reputation, partnerships, and relationships with its peers. Today, Trump is the face of America and that is a face of Danger.

1.1. The rise of Trumpism

Donald Trump's 2016 Republican Party nomination and subsequent rise to presidency relied heavily on violence, fear, hatred, threats, and division. His presidential campaign gained public traction because he displayed a unique political strategy popularly referred to as Trumpism or the Trump factor where as a candidate, Trump did not hesitate to air out his views despite how radical, or to dismantle the very core of diplomacy when interacting with fellow politicians or global partners. However, a closer look at Trumpism reveals that it is a well-engineered rightwing political campaign that is designed to cater to the racist and misogynistic American while at the same time protecting the economic interests of the wealthy.

Trumpism is founded on two specific elements. The first is that women and people of color do not belong, that they are not deserving of the rights of the White human. While this idea is not entirely new to the conservatives, the party has not been explicit with showing their racial bias or misogynistic tendencies. Then come Trump, a candidate who is not afraid to raise his voice and call Muslims terrorists or Mexicans gang leaders or drug peddlers. The Republicans of course, may have attempted to feign distress at Trump's intolerance, however, his bigotry has for a long time been what a large percentage of them think about minority groups and White Supremacists suddenly feel represented. In the end, Trump is just saying what the other Republican leaders are saying but without the subtext.

The other element is the concept of populism whereby Trump attempted to gain popularity by denouncing the elite in the society, flirting with liberal ideas while still calling out their positions and even those of some of his party members. He critiqued the current structure of the corporation and supports the protection of the lower level American by promising to penalize companies that outsourced jobs and deny opportunities to well deserving Americans. He vowed to tax Wall Street, to end the Trans-Pacific partnership (TPP), and to renegotiate the NAFTA agreements. He painted social security and Medicare as programs under threat because Americans were paying insurance for the poor and promised to protect these programs.

His political rhetoric was extremely emotion inducing with statements such as "they have robbed our working class, stripped our country of its wealth, and put that money into the pockets of a handful of large corporations and political entities" -- allowed him to exploit the fear, frustration, and anxiety that the average American had felt during the 2008 recession. This was how the concept of Trumpism rose to its popularity. He centered the ideologies of the conservative party towards the country's economic crisis and with emotive speeches that painted him as the only leader willing to do what was necessary for the country that had already been given away he managed to convince his own party members and the members of the public that only he, and his notions could restore America to the state it was in in the past. A country that owned its own businesses, and was not overrun with immigrants who only wanted to cause harm and steal the average American's job.

1.2. Is Trumpism a temporary aberration or long-term

Donald Trump has significantly changed the Republican Party and every Republican voter is aware of this. The question remains whether his notions, practices and ideologies are good for the Republican Party and the

12

future of politics. Trumpism is founded on a neoconservative adherence to economic policy from trade, foreign policy, immigration, and the size of government. It is also represented in Trump's unending demand for loyalty.

It is obvious that to some politicians, Trumpism is especially divisive and detrimental to the survival of the Republican Party and other entities that associate themselves with Trump. This is because the country, backed by globalization, better trade options, and technology continues to diversify with a significant percentage of the voter base being from minority backgrounds to whom Trump's political philosophy does not cater. Primarily, the most passionate and zealous supporters of Trump fall within the white working class for whom promises of limited immigration, reduced outsourcing, taxes, and protection of social security and Medicare worked. This implies that there is a significant percentage of the population who are especially angered at Trump's audacity and may work to ensure the eradication of his form of governance and politics.

Additionally, Trump has stood strong against the institution, be it that of the free press, the judiciary or Congress. There is significant outcry in the political, activist, and scholarly class that Trump is directing the nation towards autocracy. This is a country that has been founded on democracy and the will of people. The ideologies that Trump is propagating especially, of loyalty to him and not to the state, and his unabashed deference towards institutions that have been put in place to balance and check his actions as a president may hinder the eventual cementing of Trumpism as the new approach to political governance. His behavior alone has gone against the conventional political norms, threatening political opponents, speaking vulgarity alongside bigotry and just blatantly disrespecting the constitution.

Still, on the other hand, while Trump changed the Republican Party, he did not exactly change it into something that it previously was not. He just loudly aired what fellow Republican's often say and stand for, but without the sub text. Perhaps, there is room for more Republicans who wish to attract the white working class American in the manner that Trump did. This implies that perhaps it is a political direction that may be emulated by many. However, it is also a sure way to alienate a significant percentage of the voting class especially, if one's personality does not go hand in hand with the ideologies that they profess.

Because of these reasons, it is clear that Trumpism has received some semblance of support from a significantly small percentage of the political elite. However, the common denominator of Trumpism is Trump himself. There is a question of whether another politician will have the capability to embody the ideologies of Trump and carry them out publicly in the same way that Trump has. Additionally, the reputation of the Republican Party is currently at risk with every association to Trump. Perhaps the Republican Party is just waiting for him to go away after the end of his term because no other Republican is willing to assume the shoes that Trump will have left. Therefore, Trumpism is a short lived phenomenon that might just end with Trump.

1.3. Trump's Presidency is a Train wreck

The beginning of Trump's presidency was ablaze with accusations of abuse of power, conflicts of interest, nepotism, and voter suppression among others. Each and every year that he has been in power, Trump has managed to achieve a lower standard of leadership and become the most corrosive president in America. His presidency has been characterized by insurmountable chaos, incorrigible behavior and outrageous positions that have almost made himself and America the brunt of global comedy.

Among the first executive orders that Trump gave upon coming into power highlighted the shape of his entire presidency as one supportive and permissive of racism and violence. The order was to ban Muslims from ever venturing into the U.S., an order that he gave without adequately consulting with the affected agencies and one that resulted in the stagnation of tourism and travel. He has supported white supremacist violence against racial minorities in the country and helped to develop a country where racism is accepted.

In almost four years, Trump has managed to paint the country as an uncooperative, misogynistic and highly racist nation by destroying long and painfully earned partnerships with countries all over the world and cozying up to autocratic and authoritarian regimes. This way, Trump has alienated and blatantly insulted the countries long standing allies and threatened the democratic order of the country and the world. Alongside this, he dismissed the suspicions that Russia interfered in the 2016 elections and he selected to believe the foreign Russian president over his own intelligence agency.

Trump has disregarded the humanity of the American people by separating children from their mothers and for lengthy periods of time, caging them up in conditions unfit for human living. These conditions have resulted in death, missing family members, injuries and lifelong traumatic episodes because of this familial separation. He has unjustly supported the arrest of innocent Americans only to dismantle their lives and bring them to these inhumane conditions instead of finding better, ethical and morally upright solutions to the immigration crisis.

Instead of diplomacy and good leadership, Trump has left behind a legacy of dishonesty, ignorance, misinformation, election fraud and overall bigotry. It is a laughable situation when the president is only well known globally for his long tirades and rants on social media where he constantly spreads falsehoods that can be verified. For instance his continuous denial of climate change despite the decades of scientific evidence supporting the existence of global warming. This denial has resulted in him weakening the country's role in fighting unsustainable production.

All in all Trump has disrespected the office of the president, by using it as an attack against individuals and institutions that do not agree with him. He has instilled fear in the American people, and dismantled the trust they held for the institution of government entrusted to protect their rights. He has disregarded the country's moral standing, dishonored the democratic background of America and propagated ignorance over professionalism and the pursuit of knowledge. His presidency to date has been a perfect example of what happens when an unqualified individual is allowed to lead and it was only a matter of time until it would be tainted with impeachment calls.

1.4. Trump Totally Unchained

Trump is uncontrollable. Waldman reminds that one cannot adequately judge another's character until they witness how they treat people who push or press them. Trump is a lesson in this as a man who grew up wealthy without any obligation to anyone, who headed his own private company without any entity to oversee him and no one to question his decisions. Today, the man cannot fathom doing anything other than what he wants or being forced by a set of rules going back in history to act in a particular manner or to follow specific orders. Never has the Americas ever had a president so individualistic and narcissistic.

To Trump, only he as the president matters and so he has actively divorced himself from the traditional political conventions and disregarded the institutions that make up the American government. He has assumed his commitments to his party, alienated international allies and overall disrespected the historical figures and forces upon which the American government was founded. While this semblance of freedom and lack of care is what attracted many of his voters, it is the same thing that made the political elite and those in his party become suspicious of him. He is unpredictable and this would be a good thing if his motivations were not based on self-interest and narcissism.

He made promises to eradicate the corrupt officials from the high levels of government while he was the corrupt one. His actions have rampaged on the presidency and made many people question the legitimacy of the constitution in controlling him. From hiring his own family to work in the White House despite the existence of an anti-Nepotism Act, continuing to run his international businesses despite the Emoluments Clause prohibiting this, refusing to follow the orders of Congress to provide his financial records, to refusing to cease control of his businesses despite the conflict of interest they present with his duty to protect the American people.

Trump also appointed himself the sole determinant of who qualifies to be an American and who does not. To him, the White male working class entity is the only American deserving of rights and any other individual especially of color does not belong. He has time and again referred to people of color in biased terms suggesting that he does not understand that America was founded on immigration. Even worse is that he has not faced repercussions for his blatant stereotyping and racism against people who are not predominantly White.

His distaste for constraints has expanded to an attack against the free media. He has loudly disparaged any media house that does not report news in his favor often accusing them of misinformation. He expects a level of loyalty from everyone that he has not earned and will go on a rampage either while giving speeches or on social media against the person, media house, or institution that he believes has wronged him.

His onslaught on the different international partnerships are evidence of his unhinged personality. If he is not stopped, America is going to pay the price when it finds itself without alliances or friends. Trump has shown that he can rebel against practically anything just to show those in the room that he is in charge. He is convinced that what he is doing is correct and that is the most worrisome thing. There is a need to save America from a second term of his supreme narcissism.

1.5. Living Dangerously

There is a form of madness to Trump's presidency and policy takes that could forgive all the condemnation he continues to endure from chattering classes and opposing democrats. However, all the constraints they attempt to impact upon him are valid to protect the

American people. Since his inauguration, Trump has had a fraught four years attempting to reshape American foreign policy and only managing to shock his supposed alliances.

His main tactic for negotiation when it came to the North American Free Trade Agreement was to blow it up, or his proposed military option as a solution for the Venezuelan democratic crisis. He also promised to rain "fire and fury" on North Korea and considered going to war with one of the countries that are among the largest suppliers of oil to the U.S. Most memorable was his promise to construct a "big beautiful wall" to keep Mexicans out of the United States. Trump's approach to leadership and any form of international alliance has been bursts of promised violence that have caused the international community to revoke his unconcealed disregard for international diplomacy and his own officials running high on anxieties on what he will do next.

Since he took up office in January 2017, Trump has visited multiple countries and dined with over 100 global leaders. However, he has continued to look upon these individuals with more suspicion than he has accorded American adversaries such as Vladimir Putin and has dismantled the established norm of decorum and diplomacy. He has placed the American future at risk in more than one occasion by undermining many of the global leaders and partnerships that America has forged over the years. Perhaps Trump has a thirst for danger and that is why he acts in this manner, and for this he cannot be faulted. However, his actions come at the expense of the American people and because of this, there is need for action against him especially because it is evident that his leadership has no clear strategy in place.

Ibrahim Aldasoqi,   978-1-62265-222-8 (online) 978-1-62265-223-5 (paper)

"By the time a second term rolls around, the illusions about a president have largely evaporated."- Robert Dallek

Chapter Two: Possible Trump's Second Term in Office

Trump's possibility of a second term has the topic of much debate. However, based on the different factors, Trump's second term is imminent than we think. Irrespective of the scandals, near impeachment, and his mid-term party losses, Trump has several things in his favor. The two most notable factors are his incumbency and a good economy. To many people, Trump's second term seems far-fetched. In fact, many leaders and experts in different parts of the world wonder how the U.S. could re-elect such a president. However, after being in a recession for six to eight years and finally having a good economy, voters will not care what the world thinks. They will vote for the person that made their lives better. Trump is likely to be elected because of many factors. Some of the most notable are time and money, incumbency, and a good economy.

Therefore, if these findings are anything to go by, then the United States and the rest of the world should be ready for another four years of Trump's reign. Politicians and business people should brace themselves for similar foreign policies but a good economy.

2.1. Trump Impeachment

Trump's impeachment did not come as a surprise. It was only a matter of time given that his reign has been marred with numerous scandals. The first being Russia's interference and the Trump-Ukraine scandal. The topic of Trump and his relationship with Ukraine was among the first issues discussed by the Congressional committee. During the Trump-Ukraine scandal, Trump was accused of illegally coercing Ukraine and different other nations to give damaging reports about the 2020 Democratic Party Presidential candidate Joe Biden. Trump used proxies both in his and outside his administration among them his lawyer Rudy Giuliani and William Barr (his Attorney General) to influence the Ukrainian officials. Barr and Rudy put pressure on Ukraine to begin a probe on conspiracy theories in American politics. After a week of making his request, Trump withheld or arrested an approved military aid to Ukraine to further put pressure on Zelensky (the Ukrainian president). Believing that he would not get the military assistance they needed so bad, Zelensky made preparations to announce their investigation of Biden on CNN's Fareed Zakaria's episode which was to be aired on the 13th of September. Being informed of the whistle-blower complaint and possible leak, Trump released the aid two days before the President's announcement leading to the cancellation of the planned interview. To protect himself, Trump declassified this information and authorized the release of a transcript of his phone call with Ukraine on September 24 just a few hours before the impeachment hearings begun. The White House substantiated sections of the information released by the whistle-blower. They verified that Trump had made a call to Zelensky, and the recording of the conversation had been stored in a highly secure place in the White House, where classified information is reserved.

The witness, (Ukraine ambassador Bill Taylor and Laura Cooper), who came before the Intelligence, Oversight, and Foreign Affairs committee, said that the President might have made a call to the Ukrainian President coercing him to begin or authorise and announce their investigation on Biden and Burisma and his role in 2016 election.

On October 8, the White House responded to the House Speaker through a letter, that it would not cooperate with the investigation because the House of Representatives had not voted on the investigation and the witness interviews were being carried out in private. Nine days later, the White House acting chief of staff Mick Mulvaney while responding to quid pro quo stated that they held back the military aid based on issues related to foreign policy. However, later in the day, Mulvaney pointed out that there was no quid pro quo and that the President had withheld the military aid based on corruption reports in government.

The tensions in the process of impeachment were further heightened on October 31st when the House of Representatives voted to come up with procedures for public hearings which later began on November 13. The House of Intelligence Committee Chairman Adam Schiff stated that there was a possibility that Trump may have engaged in bribery, an offense that is punishable by impeachment.

2.2. Why Trump is likely to be re-elected

Donald Trump's presidency has been under constant criticism in the media to the point that a casual observer might conclude that Trump's re-election will be nothing short of a miracle. However, odd makers do not think so. They believe that President Trump has a solid chance of winning, especially after his impeachment. The odd makers are correct. Trump is likely to be re-elected if he chooses to run. I know that many of you may not believe this, but I will explain factors that favour Trump's second term.

2.2.1. The aspect of Incumbency

Despite Trump's negative image in the media, the concept of incumbency should not be overlooked. The United States history shows that presidential candidates who got elected are more likely to be re-elected if they vied again. It is only two presidents, Carter and Bush who lost their re-election. In the last fifty years, Nixon, Reagan, Clinton, Bush, and Obama have won their re-election despite controversies surrounding their presidencies.

A strong economy further supports the aspect of incumbency. The United States unemployment rate is at its record low. Inflation is almost non-existent while new job opportunities are being created at high speeds. Companies are now hiring while more people are opening businesses and taking advantage of a suitable economic environment. If you have ever studied presidential politics, then you know that a strong economy is one of the factors that get incumbent presidents re-elected.

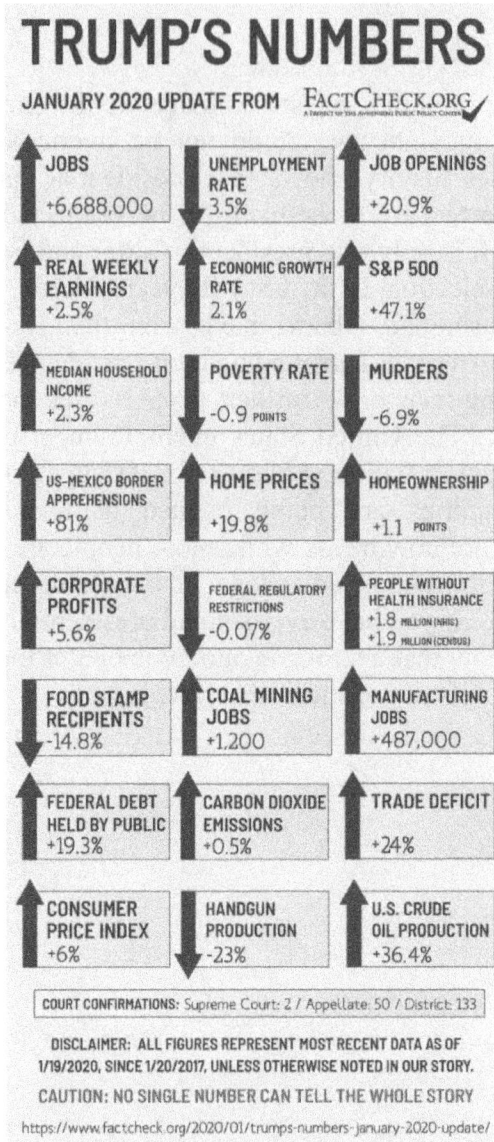

TRUMP'S NUMBERS

JANUARY 2020 UPDATE FROM FACTCHECK.ORG

JOBS	UNEMPLOYMENT RATE	JOB OPENINGS
+6,688,000	3.5%	+20.9%

REAL WEEKLY EARNINGS	ECONOMIC GROWTH RATE	S&P 500
+2.5%	2.1%	+47.1%

MEDIAN HOUSEHOLD INCOME	POVERTY RATE	MURDERS
+2.3%	-0.9 POINTS	-6.9%

US-MEXICO BORDER APPREHENSIONS	HOME PRICES	HOMEOWNERSHIP
+81%	+19.8%	+1.1 POINTS

CORPORATE PROFITS	FEDERAL REGULATORY RESTRICTIONS	PEOPLE WITHOUT HEALTH INSURANCE
+5.6%	-0.07%	+1.8 MILLION (NHIS) +1.9 MILLION (CENSUS)

FOOD STAMP RECIPIENTS	COAL MINING JOBS	MANUFACTURING JOBS
-14.8%	+1,200	+487,000

FEDERAL DEBT HELD BY PUBLIC	CARBON DIOXIDE EMISSIONS	TRADE DEFICIT
+19.3%	+0.5%	+24%

CONSUMER PRICE INDEX	HANDGUN PRODUCTION	U.S. CRUDE OIL PRODUCTION
+6%	-23%	+36.4%

COURT CONFIRMATIONS: Supreme Court: 2 / Appellate: 50 / District: 133

DISCLAIMER: ALL FIGURES REPRESENT MOST RECENT DATA AS OF 1/19/2020, SINCE 1/20/2017, UNLESS OTHERWISE NOTED IN OUR STORY.

CAUTION: NO SINGLE NUMBER CAN TELL THE WHOLE STORY

https://www.factcheck.org/2020/01/trumps-numbers-january-2020-update/

Fig. 2.1: United States Economy under Trump

2.2.2. Trump's actions against military intervention in foreign countries.

Moreover, the United States is at peace. Trump has shied from engaging in new overseas conflicts and is trying to scale back on the operations he inherited from his predecessors. Critics argue that President Trump anticipates getting out of the Middle East, especially Syria. Nonetheless, history shows that voters are not patient on foreign military intervention. Most voters have the perception that war derails a good economy and shying away from it is much welcomed. Trump has so far managed to stay away from it, giving the US the stability and prosperity it needs to be great again.

Furthermore, the aspect of incumbency is further fostered by the Democrats moving away from their blue-collar base. Winning the Democrat presidential election needs an appeal to the Left. While a large number of voters envy the wealthy and demand for more benefits, their protests decline when the economy is strong and have the opportunity to improve themselves. This is what President Trump has done. He has developed the economy and given voters a share in the economic status quo. Therefore, he can expect voter support in the primaries.

Moreover, the polls have shown a poor approval of Trump's presidency, making Democrats think that his defeat will be imminent and inevitable in 2020. Richard Nixon and Ronald Reagan also had poor approval ratings when heading to the elections. However, they ended up gunning landslide wins against their opponents. The reports and surveys showing that a large number of voters are not inclined to vote for Trump during the 2020 elections might be inaccurate given the number of historical presidential setbacks; this will be a tremendous decisive factor during the 2020 presidential polls.

Additionally, the people have gotten used to President Trump. Unlike in the past, his image has improved, and people do not view him as outrageous as they did when he became president. What this shows is that after two years as president Trump has toned down on his confrontational personality. He is not the same outsider he was when being elected. Therefore, people are getting used to his style of leadership. Trump has also learned how to modulate his leadership styles appealing to the voters effectively.

2.2.3. Immense Vetting

Trump has also been vetted thoroughly through onslaught of charges that were levied against him during the impeachment trials, and unceasingly by the media. The only thing that perhaps may still be a mystery is his tax returns. Other than that, Trump has been repeatedly questioned regarding his election, policies, allies, his actions, and his decision making. What makes him more viable is that Trump has survived all of this microscopic analysis into his every action. After overcoming the impeachment process, Trump is a known survivor and his supporters are aware that nothing can counter him after everything that he has been put through. What is even more convincing is that his track record is exactly what he promised with an economy on an upward trajectory, new trade deals with China, and he even managed to move the U.S. embassy in Israel to Jerusalem. All of these factors highlight that his supporters are not disappointed and will therefore, most likely vote for him.

2.3. Why Trump wants a second term

In his first term, Trump was fixated on specific issues that I believe are the reasons why he desperately wants a second term. First is his current engagement in the global arms race against China and Russia. Trump is motivated by a need to see the U.S. develop into the largest military power and he has taken step after step to ensure that he secures this position. From leaving the INF to increasing the military budget, I believe that the global arms race is a factor greatly motivating Trump's vie for re-election. Alongside this, is to ensure that he delivers on the big beautiful wall that he promised America. Trump has been relentlessly pushing for Congress to assign a budget to fund the wall separating America and Mexico and this is a key factor in his re-election campaign. Alongside this is his need to shrink the government. Scholars and political pundits alike have recognized Trump's seeming abhorrence with democracy and his need to transform America into an authoritarian regime. The thirst for power, may perhaps be a driver for re-election.

Trump's re-election will have several effects. The first is that the people who have not been taking him seriously will have to accept that it was not Russia that got him elected in the first place. Hence, they will have to start discussing essential matters like immigration, income inequality, and the impact of corporate America on the political world with his administration. This is because it will be imperative to find solutions to the problem before the United States falls into the trap of desperation and socialist-types of solutions. Secondly, his re-election will prompt the Democrats to start regarding him as a real president. They might decide to work with Trump in a joint plan. Trump may go ahead to compromise in several deals with the Democrats. More trade deals, for example, the replacement of the North American Free Trade Agreement with United States-Mexico-Canada Agreement might be cut with the Democrats. There might also be a massive immigration deal. Trump might even continue with his unreasonable policies, and the likes of Sanders might decide to continue engaging Trump in Russia-type conspiracies.

Ibrahim Aldasoqi,   978-1-62265-222-8 (online) 978-1-62265-223-5 (paper)

"President Donald Trump is a direct and serious threat to our country." – Rashida Tlaib

Chapter Three: The Supreme Court and Constitution after Trump's Second term in Office

This chapter is about the things that Donald Trump has been breaking and interfering with, the Constitution and the Supreme Court. It is about the most troubling and disquieting aspects about Donald Trump and his conduct as the president. Trump has disrespected these two very foundations of the American democracy, stomped on them and tried to bend them to his will. Precisely, the chapter expounds on the efforts Trump has put in place to gain control over the Supreme Court to ensure that it supports his belief that he is 'above the law.' When the Courts have gone against him, he has referred to them as "slow and political" and then worked to appoint partisan judges who believe that the president is indeed above the law into the Supreme Court. Now, the bench comprises people who are willing, against the constitutional mandates, to do as the president demands.

Even worse, has been Trump's violations of the constitution and the constitutional conventions that have dictated appropriate political behavior. From interference with elections, nepotism, and corruption to engaging in business with foreign countries that cause a significant conflict of interest with his position as the President of the United States, his duty towards the American people and his personal interests. Essentially, the Trump phenomenon while unique, is characterized by an apparent lack of understanding of the principles and values expressed in the constitution and the institutions that it establishes. The question remains, will the American Constitution, and its institutions survive the tyranny bestowed by Trump?

Ibrahim Aldasoqi,   978-1-62265-222-8 (online) 978-1-62265-223-5 (paper)

3.1. Trump Control of the Supreme Court

In the past three years, the Supreme Court has been battered and beaten to take the shape that Trump wants. Trump has time and again progressively led the public's mistrust in the Supreme Court's process by blocking, through Mitch McConnell's electoral weaponization of the nomination process, Merrick Garland's appointment to the bench, and supporting the appointment of Brett Kavanaugh despite the debacle surrounding him. Continuously, Trump has levied attack after attack on the "so called judges" as he refers to them, on the independent judiciary and the Chief Justice of the Supreme Court. Obviously, following such a targeted onslaught on the institution, it was expected to evolve into exactly what Trump wished it to be. Add in the fact that two new Justices whose appointment was directly linked to Trump and the transformation of the Court into Trump's puppet of sorts is complete.

Trump's entitled relationship with the Supreme Court began in 2016, after Antonin Scalia who served as an Associate Justice of the Supreme Court passed away. Scalia had been appointed by Ronald Reagan who was the main voice of conservative America to represent the ideals of the Republican Party in the court. At this time, it was President Obama's duty to appoint the next judge to replace Scalia. However, amidst an election year and a highly politicized process, the Senate which was made up primarily of Republican officials refused to interview the Democrat nominated candidate for the Supreme Court, Merrick Garland.

What Trump did not publicize however, was how the Senate Majority Leader Mitch McConnell blocked the nomination process. He wanted to allow time for the Republican president to take office and then nominate "one of their own." McConnell's initiative to deter President Obama's candidate was veiled in the guise of giving the American people a "voice" in the nomination process. Despite calls from the then President Barack Obama to put aside their politics and ensure a justice who demonstrated collegiality and built consensus, the senate, led by McConnell refused to interview the candidate on the basis of principle and claimed that the President's nominee was appointed to politicize the supreme court position for purposes of winning the election. To McConnell, the qualifications of the nominee would only be revised once the elections had completed and the next president was elected. The Senate held onto this position until Trump was president and on April 7th, after a relatively and laughably short confirmation process, appointed a new justice to the position, the then, 49 year old judge Neil Gorsuch. Gorsuch is as expected a conservative and adhered to the ideologies that Scalia who preceded him and Trump hold. This decision was just the beginning of Trump's attempt to reign in and take control of the Supreme Court since he took office.

Another significant situation was Trump's unrelenting support for Brett Kavanaugh in his race towards becoming a Supreme Court justice amidst sexual assault accusations by three women. Nominated by Trump, Kavanaugh represented all the principles that Trump and his conservative acolytes held dear. He had a lengthy history of ruling against regulations that hindered businesses especially those leaning towards the environment, he vehemently opposed gun control, and he held strong beliefs against reproductive rights as was shown in the Garza v. Hargan case where he denied an undocumented minority the right to get an abortion in Texas. Kavanaugh embodied exactly what the conservative side stood for. It did not matter that there was a question of the nominees' morality after he was accused by three women of sexually abusing them in the past. Trump reinforced his support for Kavanaugh even with these accusations on the grounds that even he too had been falsely accused of sexual assault and could identify with Kavanaugh. In the end, Kavanaugh, with this support from the president and a highly republican Senate, was nominated despite accusations of sexual misconduct.

These perspectives on Trump's control of the Supreme Court take on new urgency when one thinks about the most recent Supreme Court decisions and how they seem to favor the president.   For instance, when on September 18th 2019, the court allowed the government to implement the new southern border amnesty application rules that were highly restrictive. This alone was a decision that was not only unnecessary and immature, but also showed the court's direct submission to the decisions and wishes of Trump. This is a rule that was in direct conflict with the Immigration and Nationality Act that requires that "any alien who is physically present in the United States or who arrives in the United States … may apply for asylum."

Another good example was highlighted during Trump's impeachment process where he asked the Supreme Court on November 15 2019 to shield his tax returns against a subpoena levied by the Manhattan district Attorney. On this day, Trump on claims that he was "absolutely immune from all stages of a state criminal process while in office" presented a 179 page petition to the court to stop prosecutors from accessing eight years of his tax records, both personal and business related. As expected from his highly Right-winged Supreme Court, Trump's request was somewhat granted. Chief Justice

John Roberts halted the enforcement of the subpoena against Trump amidst claims of giving the Court more time to deliberate whether should be given lengthier stays in the Supreme court.

Under the control of Trump, the legitimacy of the court is coming under question. Trump has put in effort to erode the democratic nature of the court system and he poses a significant threat to the system of the government and the liberty it is bound to protect. The Trump administration has time and again ignored civic norms, encouraged anti-Semitism and racism and time and again peddled lies on different subjects. He has managed to inject this fallible perspective onto the Court system and taken control over an entity that should stand against threats to the democracy. The only question is whether this control will be durable after the end of his term.

3.2. Nepotism in the White House

For a democracy to function, the decision makers should only be loyal to the constitution and the rule of law. When those in power select or appoint their relatives who may supposedly be more loyal to them than to the citizens and institutions of government that have appointed them, then a balance against abuse of power cannot be achieved. Moreover, it is likely that those relatives do not have the relevant expertise to adequately fill the positions that they are taking and instead, the motivation to hire them is the adjudged allegiance and close connection to the individual in power. The outcome is sloppy policy making, normalization and persistence of corruption, and disregard for laws.

This is the face of Trump's Whitehouse and entire presidency. In his attempts to Trump-proof his

Ibrahim Aldasoqi,   978-1-62265-222-8 (online) 978-1-62265-223-5 (paper)

government, Trump has favored nepotism, the stamp of the authoritarian regime and tested the boundaries of the anti-nepotism law that states that a public official "may not appoint, employ, promote, advance, or advocate for appointment" a relative to an office or an agency that is run by that official. Going against this law, Trump hired Ivanka Trump, his daughter, and Jared Kushner, his son-in-law to work for him in the west wing as advisors. The Department of Justice's Office of Legal Counsel in disagreement with the nepotism call, released a statement stating that the appointment of Mr. Kushner and his wife was a legal according to a statute that exempts the president from the anti-nepotism law when hiring White House employees. Still, Ivanka Trump and Kushner are characters who were heavily involved in his campaign and he maintained that involvement by allocating them formal jobs in the federal government in the White House.

The nepotism in the president's case is especially concerning because neither Mr. nor Mrs. Kushner had any significant prior experience in policy making when they were appointed. Mr. Kushner for example, was allocated responsibilities such as solving the opioid crisis, brokering peace in the Middle East, reforming the criminal justice system, improving the government through information technology, managing diplomatic relationships with China and Mexico, and reforming veterans care. This assignment portfolio is one that Mr. Kushner has little to no experience in whatsoever, and one that will likely inhibit other qualified officials from raising their opinions in the fear of alienating the family members of the president. What is even more absurd is that the two also came with their own conflicts of interests.

Kushner for instance, did not disclose the extent of his international businesses with which he has over 100 contacts from questionable countries such as the Russian Government lawyer Natalia Veselntiskaya, and the Russian Ambassador Sergey Kislyak. During the Senate Judiciary Committee investigations into the Russian interference in the 2016 elections, Kushner did not disclose his use of private email servers or relevant emails linked to campaign documents. Moreover, Kushner and Ivanka Trump did not fully despoil from their previous business interests. In 2017, Kushner and his family sought large sums of money from Chinese investors to finance a property while his wife obtained three trademarks from the Chinese government for her brand while visiting with the Chinese president and his wife.

These conflicts of interest can be avoided only if Mr. and Mrs. Kushner removed themselves from the many issues that will be addressed by the administration. Essentially, they will be required to leave the room when the president is consulting with his advisors on the matters that arise conflicts of interest for them including real estate, trade interactions with China, taxes, or financial services. Still recusing themselves will not account for all the responsibility they hold over the policy making process. These entities still conduct businesses with foreign countries and therefore, there is a likelihood that they may put their interests first above those of the American people and run the risk of criminal prosecution.

This nepotism also highlights the president's blatant disregard for his own Ethics pledge. The White House has been especially lax in punishing ethical misconduct. There have been instances where ethical violations by Kelly Anne Conway which directly benefited the first lady were not held to the correct disciplinary standards. Because of this track record, alongside the blatant lies and falsehoods that the president himself has spewed time and again, it is less likely that going into the future, ethical misconduct by his family will be disciplined.

The currently blurred lines between what is legal and what is not regarding the issue of nepotism and hiring families in the White House may convolute the problem further and give future presidents the mandate to hire their own families, propagating a future of presidential nepotism. The future of the white house hiring process is at stake with Trump as its predecessor. There has never therefore been a more urgent need to improve on the Anti-Nepotism law as there is today. These improvements should include an amendment to prohibit presidents and other officials from appointing immediate family as White house staff, a new rule that limits the number or types of government contracts that can be held by the immediate family of a president or public official, and clarifications on clearance rules to ensure that no preferential treatment occurs for any individuals affiliated with the president and or a public official.

3.3. Disregard for the Constitution

The United States under Trump is always precipitating a constitutional crisis. Donald Trump's actions both in the country and internationally have continued to blatantly disregard the constitution and the conventions that have shaped the political arena for decades. He has time and again mocked the constitution that he swore to uphold, and another term under with him in power will guarantee that provisions in the constitution such as the Emoluments clause will lose effect. The words of our founding fathers will lose value and soon other provisions will start to lose value. The question remains whether the constitution will survive Trump's presidency.

To begin, President Trump fired James Comey, the FBI Director who had the responsibility of investigating potential criminal behavior of his inner circle and himself. What is worse is that part of the reasons that the president fired the Director was the investigation itself. In the beginning when he was fired, the president's office stated that his dismissal was prompted by the Directors mishandling of Hilary Clinton's investigation regarding her use of a private email server while she was the Secretary of State. However, publicly, President Trump acknowledged something that many observers had suspected, that the Russian investigation that the FBI was conducting, headed by Mr. Comey, was the reason why he fired him.

The FBI Director, according to the law, is allocated a ten year term to ensure that the office does not fall to political dependence. Still the president has the legal authority to fire the FBI Director for instance, one director was fired because he was accused of financial impropriety and ethical wrongdoing. Still, it is expected that criminal law enforcement agencies and their executive officers are often granted a wide range of discretion and independence when carrying out their duties. This discretion allows these criminal law enforcement agencies a structure to maintain the rule of law while overall overseen by the president, who is tasked with the responsibility of ensuring the faithful execution of laws. This authority grants the president several protections, first to have authority to ensure that all his officials are working without any influence and to ensure that an individual of integrity is appointed to that position. Additionally, as long as the president follows the constitution, he cannot be accused of any crime. Therefore, when the president violates this convention by the constitution, and takes it upon himself to eradicate officials who are investigating him, then the criminal law enforcement system ceases to be independent. So why, in a convention that greatly protects him, did Trump select to fire Comey unless he had something to hide.

Another disregard for the constitutional violation is that President Trump for years refused to release his tax returns, to an extent that in 2019, he reached out to the Supreme Court which is heavily Right winged to protect his financial documents from a subpoena. Because of this, the public has not been able to learn whether the president has had any financial connections, personal or otherwise to Russia, whether Trump was as successful a business man as he purported himself to be, whether he has been paying his taxes as required by the law or supported any charitable causes, and the level of benefit that he would assuage from his proposals to cut taxes on the wealthy folk in America. Notwithstanding these issues, had other candidates not released their taxes, then Trump could have been justified in not releasing his. However, Trump went against practice and a moral sense of obligation to withhold his tax information.

Another disregard was his violation of the Emoluments Clause that states that "No title of Nobility shall be granted by the United States: and no person holding any office of profit or trust under them, shall, without consent of the Congress, accept of any present, emolument, office, or title, of any king whatever, from any King, Prince or Foreign State." This clause was designed to shield the people who hold office in the United States from any "corrupting foreign influences." The clause prohibits federal office holders from receiving any special consideration when conducting business transactions with a foreign state.

Trump is in violation of this clause because he has stake in the Trump Organization, a multinational empire, and therefore, his financial interests and dealings with foreign countries may be motivated by personal gain and not the benefit of the U.S. Simply, his loyalties to his country and to his businesses are in conflict and this has raised questions about his trade deals and foreign interactions.. The person occupying the position of the President is expected to only have one interest, the American People. This is what should guide his decision making. But with Trump as president, Americans are afraid that perhaps decisions being made such as soldiers being deployed to wars are because Trump has stake in those countries.

His presidential orders have also been heavily against the constitution as evidenced by his initial executive order on immigration. Without vetting his order, Trump ordered a total and complete ban on Muslims from seven predominantly Muslim countries from entering the United States. This order was expected to apply to everybody entering the U.S. including tourists and was supposed to extend for ninety days and refugee admissions were suspended for 120 days. Executive orders previously were given with deference to national security and affected departments were often consulted before the order. This did not happen in the case of Trump. Instead, a poorly drafted order that was legally vulnerable and inherently inhumane to families and individuals in war torn countries and those on airplanes or abroad was passed.

In another instance, Trump disregarded the constitution by threatening his political opponent with imprisonment. The Criminal justice system should act as an independent body with its own discretion as indicated above. Therefore, politicizing the system by telling Hilary Clinton that she "would be in jail" were he to become president is a blatant disregard for the constitution. Of course once he became president he did not follow through with his threats during his campaign perhaps in accordance with the constitution that he had blatantly disregarded with the aim of enticing his crowd.

From these examples, it is clear that no public official throughout history has blatantly disregarded political conventions and the constitution as Trump has. Several instances of his progressively troubling behavior have breached the constitutional boundaries. The question remains whether, a constitution so thoroughly misused will survive a second term and if it does survive, how the post Trump constitution will be understood and used. Currently, the Supreme Court is highly conservative and if additional nominations occur, there will not exist the necessary checks and balances to ensure that the constitution is properly interpreted. Currently, as demonstrated by Trump in the examples above, the constitution has been used as a form of oppression and it is possible that the good provisions in the constitution will soon lose value under Trump.

"Donald Trump has shown no interest in working toward increasing the minimum wage, no interest in doing anything but immigrant baiting, no interest in doing anything but filling the swamp with a band of billionaires who are simply trying to help the wealthy" – Tom Perez

Ibrahim Aldasoqi,   978-1-62265-222-8 (online) 978-1-62265-223-5 (paper)

Chapter Four: US Economy after Trump's Second Term

The success of any administration is pegged on how it handles the economy and the US is not an exception. President Trump has made the US economy the centerpiece of his success in the first term. He has been relishing reports of the low rate of unemployment and steady job growth. However, in this first term that boasts of economic growth, there are raising concerns about an economic downturn that stems from Trump's escalating trade wars. Such wars threaten to undermine his economic success in the first term and put the future of America's economy in jeopardy. Trump has been making positive remarks concerning America's economy but his tenure in office is otherwise polarized. There is rising anxiety over a possible American recession not only on Trump's full glare but also after his second term. In his first term, Trump has routinely touted the growth of the US economy that largely began during Obama's tenure. Trump has touted an economic boom in his hundreds of tweets. In 2019, during his State of the Union address, Trump declared that "an economic miracle is taking place in the US." It is unfortunate that Trump has been ignoring warnings from economists concerning the prospects of a global trade war. Trump's trade practices have led to a lot of uncertainty in the future of America's economy. As the trade war continues, the US economy continues to sour. The future of the US economy is dark if all these cycles of trade war will continue in Trump's second term.

4.1. Impact on US GDP

The impact of Trump's presidency on the US GDP is both good and bad. According to Karl Smith, a professor of economics at the University of North Carolina, the good news is that since president Trump ascended to power, there has been steady GDP growth. The sentiments of Smith complement the report by the Bureau Economics. According to the 2019 analysis by the Bureau of Economics, between 2016 and 2018, there had been a steady growth of GDP which is good news.

GDP growth

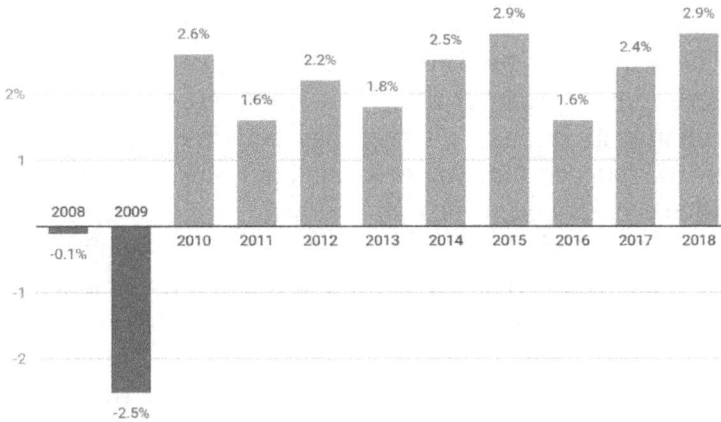

Source: Bureau Economic Analysis · Get the data · Created with Datawrapper

Fig. 4.1: Trump's impact on the U.S. GDP

The 2019 report by the Commerce Department on the strength of the US economy indicates that the US GDP has been expanding annually since 2016. In the second quarter of 2018, year-over-year GDP growth hit a peak of 3.2%. This was a stronger rebound than originally expected. Looking at the American GDP on a short-term basis, one would say that the US is doing well in terms of GDP growth. However, contrary to this microscopic view, in the long-term, there is the likelihood that the US GDP will stagger. There are compelling reasons that make one believe that the US GDP is not any good post Trump's presidency. From 2019, the growth of GDP has been slowing. Currently, the US GDP is lower than it was in the second quarter of 2015. The year-over-year GDP growth peaked in early 2018 but has since declined to levels roughly similar to that of 2015.

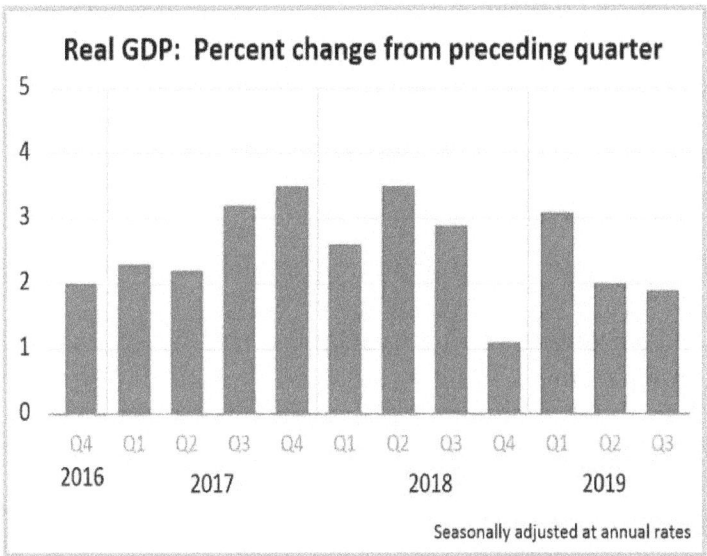

Real GDP: Percent change from preceding quarter

Fig. 4.2: America's GDP per Quarter *(Source:* Bureau of Economic Analysis)

Why would one foresee the U.S's future GDP growth from a negative perspective? Although most of the economy is consumer spending, the US business cycle is currently driven primarily by investment either in residential housing or in the business sector itself. Neither of these two investments looks good for the US GDP.

A quick review of past figures clearly demonstrates that business-sector investment is weaker than it was previously imagined. Investments on businesses strongly recovered from the 2015 slowdown but it never reached the level that it was previously estimated to be. Business investment and the overall GDP peaked in early 2018. This reflected a promising future for America but since then, it has been headed downward. The drop in GDP since 2018 began when Trump began to ramp up his trade war. Since the time Trump announced tariffs, business investments have significantly declined than expected and the trend looks to be headed towards a recessionary state in the future. If no action would be taken on Trump's tax cut and tariffs, there is the likelihood that the US GDP post Trump tenure will suffer a major blow. From the look of things, one of the major drivers of GDP-housing is also not doing well today.

According to The Economics, in 2015, the sector appeared stronger but has since been in a recessionary state since the beginning of 2018. Combined with the fall in business investments, there are reasons to worry that the US GDP may be on weaker ground than it was in 2015. Currently, according to the data by the Federal Reserve Economics, investment in housing appears to be a bigger drag on the US GDP and the US economy at large than it was previously expected. Based on the available data on the US economy and GDP growth, generally, there is a positive growth as per now but the fundamentals of GDP growth and the economy at large appears to be weaker as previously thought by economists. There is a dire need for policy change to save future America's economy and GDP. The GDP growth is likely to slow substantially in the coming years. The overall growth of GDP turned south immediately Trump ramped up the trade war. Therefore,

48

the solution to murky America's future GDP growth would be to bring the war to an end. But is Trump ready to end the trade war? Not likely.

4.2. Impact on Unemployment

In his manifesto during his campaign in 2016, Trump promised that if elected as the president, he would create more than 25 million jobs during his tenure. This appeared good in writing but practically, job creation in the US has been somehow slower under his leadership when compared to that of the end of Obama administration. Figures don't lie. According to the report by Forbes dated August 12, 2019, in the first 32 months of his presidency, Trump managed to create 5.5 million jobs. This is way below what Obama created within the first 32 months of his leadership.

President Obama managed to create 7.2 million jobs with the first 32 months of his tenure. Breaking this down to months, averagely, Trump created 173,000 jobs per month while Obama created 224,000 jobs per month. It is evident that whereas new jobs have been created during Trump's era, the rate of job creation is growing at a decelerating rate. It can thus be preempted that Trump's second term will leave America with fewer Jobs created per month if the current trend is something to go by.

Looking at the rate of employment, full-time and part-time employment gain between 2017 and 2018 was almost the same as that in 2015 to 2016. This implies that there is no much improvement in terms of employment gain when Trump's administration is compared with the immediate previous administration. When Obama's last 30 months in office is compared with Trump's first 30 months in office in terms of full-time employment, it is evident that President Obama added more to full-time employment than Trump. In terms of numbers according to the Bureau of Labor Statistics, Obama added 5.9 million full-time employments against Trump's 5.6 million. Similarly, Obama had smaller losses in part-time employment compared to Trump in a similar period. This confirms that despite the growing rate of employment in Trump's era, the rate is still lower than expected. The Bureau of Labor Statistics documents that the average number of jobs created in the first half of 2019 was 141,000. This figure is below the average jobs created per month in the years 2012 to 2018 which the Bureau of Labor Statistics approximates to be 207,000 jobs per month. Although overall, the rate of unemployment seems to reduce in Trump's era, the future is not good for the already employed persons.

According to the 2018 Economic Policy Institute report compiled by Josh Bivens and his colleagues, Trump has done more harm than good to the labor industry and several of his actions hurt workers. For instance, in 2017, Trump's action infringed employees' pay in a number of ways. Trump dismantled two key regulations that protect the workers' income especially low-to-middle income workers. He declined to defend a rule that was passed in 2016 that strengthens overtime protections for the average workers. It took a lot of effort to pass regulations that protect servers from having their tips taken by their employees. Trump has also hurt the employment environment by blocking employees to access courts because he allowed mandatory arbitration clauses in employment contracts. Trump's administration seems to fight for corporate interests rather than workers' interests.

Trump's strategy to address the issue of unemployment seems to be more of a knee-jerk reaction.

His administration took drastic measures including pursuing and detaining unauthorized immigrants as well as flagging off Temporary Protected Status for hundreds of thousands of immigrants workers. This is a temporary solution to addressing the issue of unemployment but it is inhumane and ill-advised. President Trump also rolled back regulations that protect workers' pay and safety. For instance, Trump's administration blocked the Workplace Injury and Illness recordkeeping rule. His administration also blocked the Fair Pay and Safe Workplace rule. By blocking these rules, the risks for workers are raised while companies are rewarded. The labor market under Trump's presidency is dwindling because more privileges are given to employers than employees. In this regime, companies have been awarded billions of taxpayers' dollars and this harms the working population by failing to pay minimum wages or overtime. This is a violation of important labor and employment laws and regulations.

While the future might seem bright for Americans in terms of employment rate, with these regulations in place, America will be the worst country to work in. There is the possibility of labor transfer from the US to other countries with conducive working environments. Generally, even though the unemployment level in the US has substantially declined under Trump's presidency, factors that have contributed to such decline are not permanent and with time, the looming dynamic shift is likely to surprise people with a high rate of unemployment in the post-Trump presidency.

4.3.The Sanctions on China

In March 2018, the Trump administration imposed sanctions on China. The Sanctions included restrictions on investment and tariff on products worth $60 billion. The

Sanctions on China has detrimental effects not only on China's economy but also on the US economy. Beijing vowed to take all legal measures to ensure that it protects its interests. The US sanction on China is more of a reaction to curtail China from challenging America's supremacy in technology. However, according to Trump, the imposition of sanctions on China especially the imposition of tariffs was to ensure that there is a fairground for trading. The major argument here is that China is not ready to engage in dialogue with the US hence the US sanction on China was a strategic action to defend itself from economic aggression. Economists have warned that the US action to impose sanctions on China is not good for the future of U.S-China trade relations and the loser is likely to be the US. As reported by Benjamin and his colleagues in the Guardian dated March 22, 2018, several industry groups in the US are also worried by the US Trump administration's action to impose sweeping tariffs since this is likely to trigger a chain reaction that will negatively affect the US economy even past Trump presidency. The US sanction on China was preempted to raise the cost of business between the two countries. Currently, the health of US-China trade relations is not good anymore.

4.3.1.The impact of the US-China trade war

The Trade war between the US and China began in 2018 when the US slapped China with trade sanctions. Trump has always advocated for tariffs even before he became the president. In his view, imposing tariffs was a perfect way to promote domestic manufacturing and reduce the US trade deficit. When it began in 2018, economists warn that trade war between the US and China would do serious damage not only between the two countries but to the global economy at large as protectionist actions escalate. The impact of the trade war in the US is evident. In particular, it has brought a lot of struggles for manufacturers and farmers and this has led to high prices for consumers. To other countries, it has brought collateral economic damage. The trade war between the U.S-China has led to instability in the stock market.

Currently, Trump administration is not ready to continue with the talks to remove imposed tariffs on China. If tariffs remain in place, there would be permanent economic losses to both China and the U.S. Hypothetically, when price signals are distorted, specialization that maximizes global productivity also gets distorted. There is the probability of an all-out trade war increasing although it is still low. It should be the best interest of the U.S and China to agree on issues such as intellectual property rights, market access, and joint-venture technology transfer which are the bone of contention in the U.S-China trade war. According to Senator Bernie Sanders, Trump's action to initiate a trade war with China is irrational and is likely to destabilize the world economy today and in the future.

4.3.2.Trump's Trade policies

The trade policy as laid down in Trump's Trade Policy Agenda of 2018 and 2019 is seemingly aggressive than trade policies of his predecessors. Trump argues that the focus of trade policy should be on the nation's interest thus it must be in harmony with the nation's national security strategy.   According to Trump, there is no need for America to enter a trade deal that will weaken her and strengthen its competitors.   Opinion polls have indicated that not everyone welcomes Trump's trade policies. For instance, according to the Gallup poll on the tariff the US imposed on China in July 2018, the majority of Americans believed that this was a bad policy that would destroy the American economy.

In this poll, 45% of the respondents predicted that the new policy would have detrimental long-term effects on the US economy. In contrast, 31% had a view that the trade policy would have a positive long term effect.   In the current trading environment, a majority of US citizens especially the business community is not happy with Trump's tariff policies. In particular, the US farmers are the group that has suffered major losses as a result of retaliatory measures imposed on the US by China. They are petitioning the president to remove the tariffs. Although the main interest of President Trump is to ensure that more jobs are brought back to the US, his trade policies are not any better and pose considerable risk to the economies not only to the US but also to its trading partners.

Research by the Economic Research Institutes has indicated potential job losses in the future as a result of tariff policies. To be precise, according to the research by Peterson Institute of Economics, a 25% import tax on automobiles and measures put by trading partners to retaliate such high import tax by the US is likely to result in 624,000 job losses in the US alone. Currently, instead of favoring US firms, Trump's trade policy has increased the cost of imports and the major beneficiary is the US competitors. To avoid hurting the life of future trade in the US, it is important for Trump and his administration to direct its effort in its ailing infrastructure as well as training and education as a way of strengthening its competitiveness in the international trading arena.

4.3.3. Assessing the U.S.-China relationship: Benefits and costs of the world's largest economic relationship

The US has the world's largest economy followed closely by China. However, China has the largest GDP according to the Purchasing Power Parity. It is in record that the two countries have had a cordial relationship in the past that relationship has been beneficial to both of them. The relations between these two countries sharply deteriorated under Trump's administration. Trump's administration has launched a scathing attack on China such as imposing tariffs on imports from China and banning US companies from trading with Huawei. Trump has designated China as a manipulator of currency and has imposed restrictions on visa on students from Chinese nationality. Political observers are sending a warning that Trump's trade policy is likely to result in a new cold war.

The U.S-China relation is coming to a dead end. In October 2018, Mike Pence, the US vice president issued a blistering attack on China claiming that China is using propaganda and a whole-of-government approach to advance its influence. Pence affirmed that the US will not continue cajoling and persuading China to play by the rules but will put strong and swift action that would hurt China if it continues with its infractions. China has strongly opposed US actions claiming that the US is treating it like an adversary. In all these, a cold war is coming and both the US and China will suffer economically.

4.3.4. The state of the bilateral economic relationship

The U.S-China relations in the economic sphere are played out in bilateral issues. Basically, the US bilaterally interacts with China in two basic ways. First, it interacts with China proactively through policies to make China adopt economic reforms and make it integrate into the international economy. Trump's administration considers technical assistance as the best way through which it can influence China to initiate economic reforms. Recently, the two countries created a Joint Economic Committee to work on financial reforms and system of foreign exchange. Despite the effort to maintain a healthy bilateral relationship between these two countries, there has been very little improvement especially since President Trump took office. The bilateral relations between the US and China are currently dominated by a track of reactive trade conflicts.

The trade conflict between these two countries is a result of China's rapid growth with a non-reformed economic system. According to the Peterson Institute of International Economics, the bilateral trade conflict between the US and China is associated with bilateral imbalances. The US has dominated inter-industry trade while China is a rapidly growing bilateral surplus. With these in place, fundamentals are in place for contentious bilateral relations between the two countries. According to the US Department of Commerce, the potential for China-US economic conflict is likely to worsen in the future and this will continue hurting the bilateral relations between these two countries.

The report by Congressional Research Service dated November 19, 2019, further confirms the breaking ties between the US and China under Trump's presidency. The US-China bilateral relations have been good for years but recently, the US started raising concerns over China's mischievous behavior in the trading environment. Top on the US concerns has been the direct powerful role played by China in the global economy and China's policies that require the US firms to disclose very sensitive information before being permitted to operate in China. The US, on the other hand, has set preconditions that China must meet to trade with it. None of the countries is ready to play by the set rules put forth by each country.

In a retaliatory measure, Trump's administration has undertaken policy actions such as invoking Section 301 of the 1974 Trade Act specifically to counter China's industrial policies. Trump's administration has sanctioned specific firms in China to stem economic espionage of China. As the US-China trade war continues, the bilateral relations also continue to erode. President Trump continues to raise concerns about US-China trade imbalances. There has been tension as bilateral trade talks between the US and China continues especially on financial services, agriculture, and some IP issues. Beijing has set a precondition to continue with bilateral talks and one of them is the US lifting the imposed tariffs. The future of bilateral relations between the US and China is not bright with the existing hard stance by the two countries on their trade policies.

4.4.Future of China Trade Deal

After several months of trade dispute between the US and China, the two countries signed a trade deal to ease a trade war that has rattled markets and interfered with the global economy. While speaking after signing the deal, Trump said that the deal would be transformative for the US economy. In this deal, China has promised to boost US imports above the level it was in 2017 and strengthen its rules concerning intellectual property. Despite signing the deal, observers and economic analysts argue that the deal has left many points of contention unattended. Industry leaders remain skeptical that the deal may not achieve its primary intention since a number of issues are left out of it. Vaswani Karishma, an Asian business correspondent while reporting in BBC News on January 16, 2020, highlights five things that economists, industry leaders, and analysts have confirmed to be missing in the US-China trade deal. For instance, Industrial subsidies and "made in China 2025" didn't make it in the agreement.

Made in China 2025 is a Beijing ambitious program designed to enable Chinese firms to become world-class leaders in technologies. America views this program as a direct threat to its supremacy in the tech industry. There is an outcry by the US that Chinese firms are unfairly getting assistance from the government. Although China maintains that it fairly subsidizes these companies, the fact of the matter is that with this kind of subsidy, China will gain dominance in this sector.

Secondly, the deal has not touched on the US pressure on Huawei. The US has been in the front line lobbying its allies like the UK to stop using Huawei's 5G technology services. The US alleges that China could be using Huawei to spy on customers. The US has exported bans on a number of Chinese firms and increased scrutiny on various Chinese businesses and investments abroad. The US-China trade deal talks about opening up market access, however, it remains unclear how the two countries will ensure equal market access. The US payment firms cannot effectively compete in China's financial market sector because the sector is dominated by Chinese digital payment players. Trump administration will thus have to closely monitor whether China is sincere to its commitment to treating domestic and foreign firms equally.

The origin of Trade War between the US and China has been the imposition of tariffs on China by the US. The deal that was signed has not outlined a definitive timeline on when Beijing is supposed to start seeing the reduction in tariffs. Research by the Peterson Institute for International Economics indicates that tariffs are still high-above 20% on both sides. This implies that consumers and companies are still subject to hiked payments. Overall, although there is an existing trade deal between China and the US, several gray areas are still left unaddressed. Without a doubt, the future of US-China trade health still hangs on the balance. The possibility of President Trump leaving power with eroded trade health between the two countries is high.

4.5.Can US Businessess Survive Trump

The Trump administration has introduced radical changes in business sector that both directly and indirectly affect various businesses in the US. For instance, he demanded that all US firms in China move production out of China back to the US. This move has not been taken positively by the business community in the US. China is one of the US's trading partners; therefore, an effort to fight American businesses in China is likely to negatively affect American businesses both domestically and abroad. Trump's move has made various industries and businesses grapple with rising business uncertainty. Few companies have heeded to Trump's directive but a majority of companies have vowed to stay put because such directive is disruptive to American businesses both locally and internationally. Most of the US manufacturing industries rely on the Chinese manufacturing base as an essential part of their supply chain. If trump tightens his directives on US firms in China, it is with no doubt that US businesses will not survive. A good example is Boeing-Chicago-based aircraft manufacture which has vowed to stay put in China arguing that moving production out of China is likely to push them out of business by ceding ground to rival Airbus which heavily competes in the Chinese market. Most of the US firms in China have argued that leaving China is not something they can afford and if forced, then this would be the end of most of the US businesses. The tension between the US and China has hit several US companies and businesses below the belt. Unless Trump revisits his trade policies and directives on US firms abroad, US business will collapse and will have to struggle to re-emerge in the post-Trump presidency.

Ibrahim Aldasoqi,   978-1-62265-222-8 (online) 978-1-62265-223-5 (paper)

"I don't think Donald Trump represents the Republican Party... I think more and more people are going to realize that they really don't trust him." –Betsy DeVos

Chapter Five: How Trump might shape or not shape politics in America

In the eyes of the observers such as the Organization of American States (OAS) and the Department of Electoral Cooperation and Observation among others in the political spectrum, American political health and democracy appear to be heading towards a dead end. The question that lingers in the mind of Americans is what Trump's presidency holds for American politics. Observers across the political spectrum question the capacity of various US institutions to withstand the political threat posed by Trump's presidency. Drawing on insights from American political progression and the field of comparative politics, the argument of political observers is that Trump's presidency is an intersection of erosion of democratic norms, erosion of the status of the political community, and polarized two-party presidentialism. The current political life of America is threatened due to the interactive effects of norm-breaking fueled by Trump's leadership. Political observers warn that the future of American politics seems to be trading on a dangerous ground under Trump's presidency. Trump is dangerous to American democracy due to his perpetual norm breaking.

5.1.Decline of Public trust

Trust in government institutions is important for public life and neighborly relations. However, today, when Americans think about trust, they get more worried. Trust in the federal government and political institutions by Americans has gone down especially during Trump era. The declining trust in the federal government is making it hard for the government to solve some key political problems. Presidency in any democratic country like the US is the symbol of national unity and is the foundation of the political stability of a given nation. The President plays a role in shaping the political future of a given nation. The responsibility of the president is to build a political landscape that is promising and anchored on democracy. However, Trump through his political rhetoric seems to have deviated from the political norm and champions for his personal agenda rather than building trust in political institutions. This makes Trump a dangerous person to hold the highest position of power in the US.

As Written by Karen in Foreign Affairs magazine dated February 2018, Trump started destroying the future of American politics and presidency by alleging that he would make America great again because he has now turned to be a threat to various political institutions. Public opinion polls have consistently indicated that a good number of Americans have no trust in Trump's leadership and regard him as a person who cannot be trusted in a number of ways.   Even in the global context, things are not any better since the majority of US allies including France, Germany, Japan, Jordan, South Korea, the United Kingdom, and Australia all do not have confidence in Trump and believe that Trump is pushing the American political future towards a wrong direction.

Trump suffers a credibility gap not only in the eyes of Americans but in the eyes of global allies. As documented in the New York Times, political analysts argue that in his first 40 days in office, Trump uttered at least one untrue word every day. His actions speak louder. He described NATO, the US oldest and most important commitment as an "obsolete" entity. He later recanted the sentiment after witnessing uproar from citizens and US allies. Although the US does not derive its political credibility from the words of executive alone, the behavior of the president carries a lot of consequences. As Trump undermines the nation's political credibility both at home and abroad, citizens and allies continue to lose trust in the American political system. There is a high likelihood that Trump will leave America politically polarized than he found it due to his radical political decisions making.

5.2.The current and future of US politics in regard to Trump attempted impeachment

President Trump is the fourth president to have attracted impeachment debate in the history of the US. For the impeachment debate to be instigated against a sitting president, that president must have violated the norms and safeguards that are meant to protect the interest of citizens from corruption and misdeeds in the topmost office on the land. Although Trump survived the impeachment by the Senate, the whole issue is still alive in the minds of Americans and it means a lot to the future of US politics and leadership at large. The political implication of any attempt to impeach a president is twofold. First, it demonstrates a collapse of the presidency and a lack of public trust in the highest office on the land. Secondly, it demonstrates the failure of a given political party to stand firm by its manifesto and protect the interest of the people.

Taking the former, although Trump survived impeachment, the attempt in itself is likely to redefine American politics especially the conduct of the president while in office. It is likely to shape the future of the American presidency as an institution. The debate on Trump's impeachment was instigated by his actions including violation of certain norms that are in place to safeguard presidency as an institution. President Barrack Obama finished his two terms without being involved in any impeachment debate. In contrast, his successor in his first term survived impeachment. This indicates that Trump's integrity is questionable. Trump's attempted impeachment stands as a warning signal to other politicians who would want to ascend to the highest office on the land that presidency requires high level of integrity and that no one can violate the constitution and go scot-free. Impeachment of a president can have significant effect on the political party that sponsored the president. For instance, in this case, American citizens trusted the Republican Party and gave it the mandate to lead and protect their interests. The debate on his impeachment thus reveals that the Republican Party somewhat failed to sponsor a candidate that can change the American political landscape for better. Therefore, although he survived impeachment, the attempt in itself reduced the ratings of the Republican Party which must work hard in the future to re-build its reputation.   If the Republican Party fails to act immediately, the attempted impeachment of their presidential candidate is likely to send the party into opposition for a longer period in the future.

It may be fortunate to some and unfortunate to others that Trump survived impeachment but all in all, his rating has gone down. He continues to lose public support and this is something that is likely to send his administration into historical book of poor leadership. The bad reputation Trump has created in terms of leadership is likely to reenergize Democrats who are likely to find their way to power and get the opportunity to reverse most of Trump's outrageous policies. Within his first term, Americans have begun to call for reforms in various sectors due to Trump's outrageous policies. President Trump's impeachment would have likely ended the Republican flirtation with extremist politics but his failure is still ripe and alive. Post-Trump presidency will be characterised by various reforms that are likely to restore American reputation before its global allies. The polarization of American democratic norms began before Trump's presidency but has escalated during his era. A call to restore sanity and democratic norms is inevitable.

5.2.1 What is likely to happen if Trump wins the second term?

The future of America is darker if Trump gets the opportunity to be reelected. Trump's impeachment has failed, therefore, there is the likelihood of a pro-Trump GOP retaining the presidency and both houses of Congress are likely to rally behind him. Trump has the opportunity to gain a solid majority of the Supreme Court now that he has rejuvenated following survival from his impeachment. He is likely to play around with the constitution to create a durable white electoral majority. This would be made possible through a combination of immigration restrictions, large-scale deportation, and the adoption of strict laws on voter ID that he had earlier initiated. Trump's survival is likely to culminate and reengineer the electorates which would be accompanied by the elimination of the filibuster and other rules that give the Senate minorities protection so that it becomes easy for Republicans to push for their agenda even with a narrow majority.

Such measures appear extreme but are most probable if Trump wins the second term in office. Democrats will not take the efforts to strengthen the Republican Party by way of engineering a new white majority lightly because it would be an effort that would be profoundly anti-democratic. Therefore, Trump's second term is politically disastrous. A post-Trump future from a distance is characterized by polarization and a departure from unwritten political conventions. This is possible following Trump's actions and policies in his first term.

5.3. Voting Values

The 2020 presidential election is around the corner but a majority of Americans report a high level of dissatisfaction with the electoral process. According to the 2019 NPR poll, the majority of Americans believe that Trump is the masterpiece of election interference. In this poll, 41% of Americans believe that the US under Trump's presidency is not prepared to keep the forthcoming election safe and secure. President Trump himself is alleged to be the victim of election interference. It is alleged that in 2016, Russia interfered with the presidential election in favor of President Trump.

This allegation has soiled the American electoral process where a good number of citizens now say that there is no value in voting. A majority of Americans view the American electoral process to have been attacked under Trump's leadership. They view this attack as the biggest assault on the sovereignty of the US. President Trump has done nothing to reassure Americans that the country's electoral process is safe and free from attack. Trump seems to be aware of electoral fraud and benefits from outside forces influencing American elections. The alleged electoral interference by Russia is still fresh in the minds of Americans. Going forward, without proper mechanisms to maintain the integrity of the electoral process, it is most likely that Americans will not trust any future electoral processes in the US and voting will lose its meaning in the American elections. A survey by NPR indicates that 4 out of 10 Americans have lost faith in the voting process and view voting as valueless.

A similar poll conducted by The Hill-HarrisX in 2018 indicates that the majority of Americans have lost trust in the electoral process. Although there is no substantial evidence that foreign power interfered with the American voting process in 2016, about 4 in 10 Americans still believe that there is a likelihood of another country interfering with votes cast in subsequent elections to change the result in favour of a particular presidential candidate. The result of the polls painted a picture of a polarised electoral process and it would be difficult to convince the small percentage of Americans that have lost faith in voting and the American electoral process in general. Although election officials and intelligence are working round the clock to reassure voters about the integrity of the electoral process, the public still raises a concern about the effect of disinformation in the political discourse. Those who have already lost faith and trust in the US electoral system continue to intoxicate others and in the future, Americans will completely lose trust in the voting process and voting will be meaningless in the eyes of Americans. Trump being involved in the allegation of electoral interference has soiled his name and this makes him a dangerous person to hold a top most political office.

5.4.United States unity under Trump

The unity of Americans has always been unstable due to different factors including race and ethnicity. The US in the past and even currently experiences polarization of unity brought about by racial discrimination and that resulted in divisive politics. When President Trump ascended to power, some of his policies such as immigration policy further polarised the nation along racial lines. Trump policy seems to favour whites than other races. His immigration policy has compounded the problem of disunity among Americans. However, in his speech on February 5, 2019, he urged Americans to come together and get united as one nation.   While addressing Congress, he said, "*We must reject the politics of revenge, resistance, and retribution — and embrace the boundless potential of cooperation, compromise, and the common good.*" Trump had realized that Americans stood divided under his leadership than before.   By promising to do something about American disunity and transforming himself into a bipartisan public leader, he already knew that his leadership is characterized by ethnic polarization and racial discrimination. The opposition has rejected Trump's overture arguing that his policies are compounding the problem of disunity among Americans. Trump's second term is likely to be characterized by further polarization of American unity if some of his policies such as immigration policy that target particular races are not mitigated. Trump's radical stance on ISIS is doing more harm than good to Muslim-Americans. His theatrics has made Muslims in the US to be branded as terrorists and this together with some of his racist remarks have escalated ethnic polarization.

5.5.Civic Membership and Status

American civic health since the 1970s has been in steady severe decline but today, millions of citizens that for a long time have been bystanders are taking part in civic education. Trump would be echoed for giving room to civic membership such as League of Women Voters to grow. President Trump has given communities that have long been disregarded by cosmopolitan political elites a voice to reason and these people are now rallying to his defence. Civic education has received a boom under Trump's presidency and across the country; citizens are creating discussion circles and political clubs. The civic surge under Trump's presidency is good on one side and bad on the other side because it crosses ideological lines. For instance, branding Muslims as undocumented citizens has given them a civic status that every American will look down upon as a dangerous group. Trump has constantly trivialized Muslims in the US subjecting them to exclusion. With this kind of branding and allowing for civic status dubbed "us versus them" the future of American is not any good. Trump is sowing a culture of hatred among various civic groups by commending some groupings and trivializing others.

Ibrahim Aldasoqi,   978-1-62265-222-8 (online) 978-1-62265-223-5 (paper)

"To say Donald Trump would be a disaster for our country, our democracy, and our future would be doing a grave disservice to the word 'disaster'." - Tom Steyer

Chapter Six: Trump contribution to declining American Democracy

America is among the strongest democracies in the world. The Founding fathers designed it this way, to be strong and durable with checks and balances to prevent any one individual or branch of government from gaining too much power. Three years under Donald Trump and these checks and balances are all under threat, and the core value of democracy itself has been eroded. In this chapter, the basic markers of democratic decline and Trump's role in propagating them are identified. They include: politicizing independent institutions, spreading disinformation, quashing dissent, amassing executive power, corrupting elections, and delegitimizing communities.

Throughout his presidency, Trump has made a series of decisions that have propagated these markers of democratic decline, and also added new threats to the democracy. What he is doing is developing an authoritarian play book to eliminate freedom in the country and amass unending power for himself. These are actions that are especially similar to what countries with declining democracies in the world such as Turkey and Venezuela have been taking.

The chapter also highlights the effects that Trump's actions have on the liberal democracy, especially with his blatant disregard for the political system and the constitution. Essentially, The United States is a liberal democracy, an antithesis of authoritarianism. It is supposed to be founded on free and fair elections, freedom of speech, an independent judiciary, media freedom, civil liberties, minority rights, the rule of law, and a system of checks and balances that prevent the concentration of power. Trump's presidency has taken these elements and institutions of liberal democracy and eroded them for instance through distorting truths, attacking the media, influencing the federal judiciary among others. Essentially, it is evident that the U.S. democracy may not survive the Trump presidency.

6.1. Anti-democratic Tendencies

The American democracy came under threat the moment Trump became the president of the U.S. The president's unorthodox actions and decision making processes make up a story of a president who has unsettling autocratic tendencies that threaten the very core of the American nation, its democratic base. Following a first term filled with misinformation, de-legitimization of communities, dysfunctional independent institutions corrupt elections, and crushed dissenting opinions, it is worrisome that American will cease to be the strongest democracy in the world under the continued leadership of Trump. In this part of chapter 6, I will highlight the six markers of democracy and Trump's actions against them.

6.1.1.Politicized independent institutions

Healthy democracies function under independent institutions free from any political influence or control. Institutions such as law enforcement systems and the civil service must operate with some level of insulation from the impulses of political leaders and maintain a semblance of discretion alongside their independence. The aim is to constrain the leaders who are power hungry and would use them to gain more control over the people. These systems have been put in place to enforce, and execute the constitution of the country based on evidence and facts. In line with this, the Justice Department in the US, alongside

73

a multitude of other federal agencies are expected not to be involved or used to promulgate partisan politics. Civil servants in the U.S. take their vow not to the president but to the constitution and the people of America and often they hold their position in different governments.

Sadly, Donald Trump has not tried to uphold the values of respect that these institutions demand. After the outcome of the elections an inquiry into his presidential campaign that alluded that he had colluded with the Russian government to win the elections began. However, in a bid to obstruct justice and prevent further investigation, Donald Trump fired the then Director of the FBI James Comey who was leading this investigation in 2017. Alongside this, he worked to weaken the federal bureaucracy by threatening his perceived enemies, leaving government positions without holders, cutting agency budgets and diminishing the public's trust in its public servants by highlighting them as biased and disloyal.

6.1.2.Misinformation

In a democracy, accountability founded on truth enables the creation of a functional government. The core of this is, enshrined in the First Amendment of the constitution as a free press whose role is informing the public about their leaders and the decisions they are making. However, Trump has sought time and again to constantly assault the truth and the capability of the American people to discern truths from falsehoods. Trump has time and again harassed journalists, discredited the press, dismissed any sources of information that favors others, and threatened to subpoena reporters and change libel laws when reports about his activities regarding not just public policy and current events, but also his personal life are brought to light. Additionally, this president has time and again indiscriminately spread lies and publicly disputed scientific facts such as issues of global warming all of which undermine his credibility.

6.1.3.Executive power

The US democracy thrives from a separation of powers in government. In a functioning balance and check system, the judiciary and the legislature stand in the way of an executive having too much power. Donald Trump has sought to undermine this system by first attacking the judiciary, then appointing only conservative judges to the Supreme Court such that people who hold similar ideologies as himself are in decision making positions. Additionally, he has constantly disregarded the role and powers of the Congress, treating it as a subordinate by withholding information, especially his financial records after they were requested, refusing to consult with the house and acting according to his own will especially on matters regarding international trade, and he has constantly punished states that have opposed the policies that he presents.

6.1.4..Quashed dissent

A democracy thrives on opposition and the vibrant dissent. This is because those in opposing positions provide the public with alternative policies and solutions and prevent the abuse of power by leaders. Authoritarian leaders are often the sole attackers of dissent and Trump's actions highlight his dictator tendencies. Trump has displayed no tolerance for any individuals who disagree with him and he has constantly threatened his opponents with loss of employment and imprisonment. A good example is when he threatened to jail Hilary Clinton his opponent during his political campaign. The result of this is that a culture of fear has grown in the government because people suddenly fear speaking out against him.

6.1.5.Corrupt elections

Americans have the right to choose who governs them and this is the greatest threat to autocratic leadership. Trump has time and again demonstrated his blatant disregard for the American electoral process stating even before he became president that he would reject the outcome of the elections if he lost. After becoming president Trump has continuously refused to protect the legitimacy of this process by not condemning Russian interference in the 2016 electoral process, firing the FBI director in charge of the investigation into this interference and not placing necessary measures to prevent recurrence of the interference.

6.1.6.Delegitimizing minority communities

America was founded on immigration and it thrives on diversity. Most leaders have time and again expressed their interest and support for inclusivity and diversity in America in a bid to keep up with the changing times and attempt to absolve the country of its imperfect history against minorities. Still, Trump has exhibited his intention to attack minorities not just in his words but also in his actions. For instance, after becoming president, he put out an executive order banning the entry of Muslims from 7 countries into America. Trump has also tried to appeal to the divisive and hateful history of the country by scapegoating specific minorities and inciting hatred against them. As a result, racial, sexual, religious, and ethnic minorities have continuously faced violence and discrimination from the white opponents who believe these lies. For instance, the idea that Muslims are terrorists, or Mexicans are drug dealers and gang members. Moreover, Trump has been reluctant to condemn this violence which has made the perpetrators bolder with their attacks and their ideologies that people of color are not true Americans.

6.2. Trump and the issue of Liberal Democracy

There is a constant fear that the U.S. is on the edge of a regime change of course amplified by Trump's presidency. Today many scholars, citizens and activists are actively afraid for the future of the American democracy. In 2016, a survey conducted by the Pew research institution indicated that already, concerns about the American democracy was growing as many reclassified the country as a flawed democracy instead of a full democracy. This was of course caused by the diminishing confidence in political institutions and increased pessimism in the system as a whole.

However, since Trump took reign as the president, these doubts have magnified tenfold. Initially as a candidate and today as the president, Trump blatantly disregards the core foundations of democracy in the US from the free press, the bureaucracy, the electoral process, the opposition and the judiciary. Trump has also shown great support for white supremacy whose members have mobilized and gained immense support and voice since he became president. His selected method of governance also challenges the democratic liberalism that comes from institutional commitments and impactful policies. Internationally, he has crashed time and again with the democratic alliances that the US has spent decades forging and out rightly demonstrates his admiration for autocratic rulers such as North Korea's Kim Jung Un. Moreover, very early into his first term as president, Trump botched a criminal investigation designed to uncover the role that the Russian government played in the 2016 elections and the connections they had to his campaign.

It is therefore clear that the presidency of Trump on all these facets has diminished the integrity of the political system in America, and its resilience to ever function as a liberal democracy once again. Concern raises from voters, politicians, activists, and even scholars. Some of these entities believe that just like in the past, when the political institutions faced immense threat due to the actions of their politicians, for instance during the Watergate scandal, the democracy and political system still recovered. However, when thinking about Trump, to many, the future is bleak because Trump is not the normal political being and he does not subscribe to the normal political conventions or traditions. There is no telling where his motivations are placed because they are very clearly not on the maintenance of a democratic process.

This is best demonstrated in the civic membership and status questions that Trump's presidency has presented again. Suddenly questions of who has the right to participate in politics and even just in the community have arisen again and with them the blatant disrespect and discrimination of those they perceive to not belong. From history, liberal ideas have been very conflicting with the American traditions that were put in place. Often these conflicts arose with regard to issues concerning race, gender, religion, ethnicity, historical background among others and the political contests that have taken place throughout history between the liberals and the conservatives have greatly defined politics and the development of the nation.

The racial structure of America for instance, and identity characteristics that have just recently been brought into political conversation among others have shaped the conflict over civic membership and in turn the political structure.   Trump has embraced the racial animosity, disregarded liberal perspectives in different policy initiatives such as reproductive rights, gun control, and immigration among others. He has also supported the ascent of anti-democratic politicians into the political arena and transformed the judiciary into a conservative body. Currently, under the Trump administration, the balance and checks that come with an apt opposition and a powerful legislative body and judiciary have been dispelled.

There is a fear in the future of American liberal democracy and the fear is castigated by the destruction of democratic norm at the mass and elite levels. A combination of polarized two-party presidentialism and the eroded democratic norm has produced a new arrangement that is totally different from the past moments of crisis in the history of American politics. In the current political sphere, it is important to take an analytical approach to Trump's leadership and draw insights from comparative politics and the traditions of political development in America. Generally, Trump's presidency has changed American politics. It thus implies that the fundamental feature of the American democratic form of government, as well as the American political order that underlies the American democratic norm, is at risk.   The continuation of these changes should be taken with deep consideration.   The transition of the democratic norm from the current regime to the next regime is likely to meet hurdles because the foundation of democracy appears to have been weakened further under Trump's presidency. Liberal democracy is the cornerstone of American democracy and it stems from American ideology but it is a form of democracy that has been threatened by various regimes and worse in Trump's era and this is likely to be pushed into the subsequent regimes.

6.3. Erosion of United States Democracy

The long term stability of the U.S. and its political scene greatly depends on a particular set of norms, informal but commonly held by all politicians. This set of rules governs the behavior of the politician when the formal rules are not at work. The rules are often self-explanatory from ensuring mutual respect with the houses, and across party lines, tolerating vigorous dissent from opposition, and respecting the electoral process among others. However under the tyranny of Trump, things are slowly changing.

Historically, Democracy was a procedure that helped to manage any conflict by institutionalizing it. The forefathers were deliberate in their design of the governmental structure. They organized the administration in a way that would make the contest for power a routine while at the same time checking the political power one individual or group held. Balances and checks to be simple that fostered and at the same time controlled the government function. The aim was to ensure that a dictatorial rule motivated by a need to take over the power from the citizens was prevented. This system has of course changed over the past centuries that America has been sovereign. Still, the restraints placed on institutions and processes have been resilient and have constantly bound the politicians to their conventional norms and behaviors while at the same time, instilling a set of expectations in their citizens on how the democracy should look like and should function.

The problem however, is that recent developments, spurred on by the actions of today's president Donald Trump, have taken to rapidly eroding this very core and discriminating against the very intentions of the founding fathers. Globally, the room for free speech, and competitive politics is getting smaller and smaller as autocrats attempt to push back democratic norms. A good example of this is the collusion between Trump and the communist Russian government to manipulate the election results in 2016, and his blatant disregard for independent institutions when he interfered with the FBI investigation and fired James Comey, the FBI director.

Trump's actions clearly indicate that he questions the idea of democracy, how and why it is promoted. Trump has openly criticized the US foreign policy, and questioned the U.S. intent push for the democratization of countries. He claimed that it is a dangerous idea to attempt to make democracies out of countries that do not wish to become democracies or have no experience in running as democracies. He has called American policies illogical and arrogant and to him, this is the policy that greatly strengthened ISIS. This is a position that a president has never taken because it clearly questions the appeal of achieving universal democracy where all citizens take a significant role in their governance. He cemented this idea by highlighting that America's democracy had derailed and therefore, the U.S. was in no place to guide others on democracy. Given his stance on democracy, it is no wonder that upon his inauguration, he did not appoint any senior level officials who are proponents of democracy, or when his selected secretary of state attempted to reduce the budget for democracy and governance.

Trump is attempting to slowly but surely discredit America as a democratic nation and as the face of the country, his actions only highlight this. He has distanced himself from protecting his minority citizens from violence and instead propagated white supremacy, he has raised doubts about different institutions, he has attacked the media and he has openly embraced leaders who are authoritarian, North Korean and Russian leaders. Trump has not shied away from expressing his racism and sexism and he has made his slogans based on the defamation of entire communities, populations and religions. This is a problem because he is slowly creating a normalcy of hatred and phobias in his countrymen that a certain group of people is not to be trusted and should therefore not be allowed into the country. Only a good percentage, that is the White people, are trustworthy and only they should be participating. This has resulted in violence against the country's citizens and blatant voter suppression.

Trump is also attempting to normalize the disregard for other branches of the government that have been put in place to balance political powers. Most especially the Congress. Trump has time and again disregarded direct orders from Congress in an 'I have the right to do whatever I want I am the president' mentality. He apparently believes that being the president absolves him from taking responsibility for his actions or responding to the orders made by Congress. This is especially worrisome because any provision from the constitution that has granted the Congress powers places the liberties and the rights of people at risk. Trump is somewhat giving future leaders the leeway to act however it is that they wish as long as they are president which in itself is wrong because disobeying orders from Congress constantly weakens the institution that was put in place to protect the American public from lawless behavior from their leaders.

Ibrahim Aldasoqi,   978-1-62265-222-8 (online) 978-1-62265-223-5 (paper)

All in all, it is evident that from the partnerships Trump makes, the ideologies of hate against minorities he preaches, the disregard for established institutions and free press are all small steps he is taking towards normalizing authoritarianism in the country. The changes are subtle but they are there and a second term of this trend will see the great states of America fall into the control of a bigoted and irrational president and his foreign similarly inhumane friends.

"I believe that there's a change in weather and I think it changes both ways"- Donald Trump

Ibrahim Aldasoqi,   978-1-62265-222-8 (online) 978-1-62265-223-5 (paper)

Chapter Seven: Trump actions leading to irreversible Climate change

Trump's position on climate change had been wavering before he became the president and this extended even during his tenure as the world's most powerful man. Trump has been a fierce critique of climate change activists terming them as "prophets of doom", something that has attracted public debate on what he stands for in terms of climate change. President Trump's actions are not in support of fight against climate change which other nations of the world are fighting against and this is dangerous for the future of the world.

Trump's sentiments at the World Economic Forum in Davos clearly indicate that he is less in support of fight against climate change. Trump on the one hand, dismissed "alarmists" saying that their intention is to "control every aspect of human life" while, one the other hand, he expresses the support of the US for the initiative to plant a trillion trees to curb the issue of climate change. If one would then judge Trump based on his words on climate change, his views appears to be not only confusing but also contradictory. On the one hand, he uses derogatory terms such as *"mythical" "nonexistent" or "an expensive hoax"* to refer to climate change while on the other hand; he describes climate change as a *"serious subject"* that should be looked into with great attention. Furthermore, it is very easy to tell Trump's position on climate change following his series of tweets and opinion on newspapers on the subject.   For instance, in 2009 before he became the president, he expressed a formidable support for legislation to combat climate change in the New York Times.

In particular, his statement read, "*If we fail to act now, it is scientifically irrefutable that there will be catastrophic and irreversible consequences for humanity and our planet.*" Surprisingly, in the years to follow, he took a different approach and in a series of *Twitter* posts, he made the issue of climate change insignificant. For instance, in 2012, Trump referred the problem of climate change as a vice choreographed by the Chinese to discredit US manufacturing and make it non-competitive. Years later, he recanted the statement claiming that it was a joke.   For instance, in January 2020, he said, "*Nothing's a hoax about that. It's a very serious subject... I want the cleanest air, I want the cleanest water. The environment is very important to me. I also want jobs. I don't want to close up our industry because somebody said you have to go with wind.*"   But that aside, he has regularly claimed that scientists' rebranding of "global warming" to "climate change" is a strategy to hoodwink people and blow the issue out of proportion.

However, experts at NASA have countered his argument saying that climate change is the right scientific and accurate term. In another series of tweets, Trump has suggested that climate change has been disapproved by cold weather. This is despite the fact that the World Meteorological Organization has said that the world in the past two decades has experienced the warmest temperatures and this is likely to be experienced in the years to come. In the recent past, Trump has tweeted less on the issue of climate change and since his election as the US president, he has adopted a wavering and ambiguous stance in speeches and interviews. Trump tends to frame the issue of climate change in regard to clean air and water or the cost to businesses. This has no direct relationship with climate change. For instance, in December 2019 he said, *"Climate change is very important to me. I've done many environmental impact statements in my life, and I believe very strongly in very, very crystal clear clean water and clean air."* This leaves people to question Trump's belief and position on climate change.

7.1. Climate rising at increasing proportions

The significant effects of climate change are already noticeable in the environment both in the US and globally. Today, the rate at which Ice on rivers and oceans is melting is higher. The rate at which glaciers shrink is worrying. The rate of flowering is also higher with a significant shift in plant and animal ranges.   Scientists in the past forecasted the possible effects of global change in climate and today, the effects are evident. Today, people experience more intense heatwaves, accelerated rise of sea level, and loss of sea ice. There is sufficient evidence which indicates how the damages caused by climate change are likely to be significant and are likely to worsen in the near future. Scientists continue to send signals about the possibility of the rise of global temperatures in the next coming decades due to an increase in the amount of greenhouse gases released to the atmosphere as a result of human activities.

The forecast by the Intergovernmental Panel on Climate Change (IPCC) on change in temperature indicates that there is a possibility of the rise in temperature of approximately between 2.5 and 10 degrees Fahrenheit over the next 100 years. This panel comprises over 1,300 scientists drawn from various parts of the world including the US. The report by the IPCC indicates that the extent of the effects of climate change on specific geographical areas is likely to vary with time. The effect will also vary with respect to the environmental and societal systems ability to adapt to change. IPCC has documented the expected effects of climate change in the future including high temperatures, prolonged season of frost-free, changes in the pattern of precipitation, an increased pattern of drought and heatwaves, stronger and more severe hurricanes, Arctic becoming Ice-free and the rise of sea-level by about 1 to 4 feet. The regional effects of global warming are imminent. The report by the Third and the Fourth National Climate Assessment reveals that in Northwest, there is a noticeable rise in sea level, erosion, and increasing wildfire. In Southeast, there is a noticeably decrease availability of water and extreme heat while in the Midwest; there is extreme heat and noticeable heavy downpours. In Southwest, there is increased heat, drought, and noticeable insect outbreak as well as declining water supply. All these changes are of great concern to the US people but what is Trump's take about them?

Trump seems to be less concerned about what climate change can result in, both to the US and to the world at large. According to Michael Gerrard, a professor of environmental law at the University of Columbia, President Trump lacks understanding of what climate change entails and its impact on the US and the world at large. Joseph Goffman, executive director of Harvard's Environmental Law Program also hinted that Trump does not believe in climate change. He described him as a "climate nihilist." President Trump considers the issue of climate change as political instead of considering it as an environmental and moral issue. Various reports on climate change have repeatedly indicated that, indeed, it is a threat to humanity and it is changing too fast in this century. IPCC continues to warn about the effects of climate change in the coming decades and calls for mitigation efforts sooner than ever. As the global superpower, the US has a role to play in climate mitigation but without the support of the president, such efforts cannot see the light of day. It is unfortunate that despite the fast speed in which climate change is taking place, Trump and his administration continue to give little attention to it and continue to politicize most of the things about climate change. What such actions hold for the future of America and the world at large is indeed miserable!

7.2. Trump's stance on Climate Change

I have said repeatedly that Trump's position on the issue of climate change is unsteady. According to him, climate change is not as a result of human activity. Trump appears to disregard the overwhelming scientific evidence which suggests that the global temperatures have increased in the recent past courtesy of human activity. He believes in the clean environment- clean air and water but has little belief about climate change. Trump's actions confirm that he is not in support of the idea of climate change. For instance, following his election as the US president, a large amount of information regarding climate change had been removed or altered on the EPA website. This act was a major setback to the effort made by the coalition of scientific and academic groups that made several copies about climate change on the EPA web pages. In his first year in office, more than 200 web pages that provide information about climate change were either deleted or omitted. Several pages were altered by removing mentions of climate change.

In June 2019, Dr. Rod Schoonover, the US State Department analyst tried to testify to Congress concerning the probable catastrophic effects of climate change and the role played by human activities in fueling climate change.

Unfortunately, Trump's White House reportedly tried to block him from making such an address to Congress. Trump's White House reportedly blocked the testimony written by Dr. Rod from being incorporated into the official Congressional Record claiming that Rod's report was uncoordinated and was not the official position of Trump's administration. The report by Schoonover was criticized also by the National Security Council claiming that the report had very little truth in it. To further compound the problem, the White House Office Legislative Affairs came up with a proposal to remove Schoonover's five testimonies about the scientific baseline of climate change and the contribution of human activity in fueling climate change.

President Trump has softened his rhetoric about climate change but continues to talk about climate change in a more general environmentalist term. He has not come out boldly to denounce his previous rhetoric on climate change. Political analysts argue that a change in tone on Trump's stance concerning climate change is likely to be for political reasons. He is much aware that his negative stance on this issue can significantly affect his political survival. As a result, he has changed the tone to win the heart of the majority of Americans who believe that climate change is a global problem that requires immediate mitigation strategies. A survey conducted by Pew in 2019 found that 52% of young Republicans had a feeling that climate change is real and the government was doing little to rescue the situation. A survey by the American Conservative Coalition indicates that about 67% of Republican voters feel that Republican Party should stand to defend the country against the forthcoming catastrophic effects of climate change. It is because of these survey results that Trump has changed his tone and stance about climate change purposely to be reelected. It is quite unclear whether he will stick to his tone in the future. America being the superpower, being led by a person who does not care about the issue of climate change is dangerous to its future. These having been said, it is predictable that the world after Trump's presidency might be the most dangerous world.

7.3.Regulatory roll-backs

There are several steps that have been taken by Trump's administration to scale down measures that had been placed to fight climate change. This further proves his lack of interest in the fight against climate change. High-profile rollbacks include the decision made by his administration to make the US not a party to the Paris Climate Agreement, replacing President Clean Power Plan initiated by Obama with a new rule; the Affordable Clean Energy rule, and an attempt to freeze the standards of fuel efficiency imposed on new vehicles as well as preventing California from setting its own emission rules. Trump in person stood and announced the US withdrawal from the Paris Agreement on June 1, 2017. The US had previously pledged to reduce the emission of greenhouse gas by 28% and assigned $3 billion to be used by foreign countries to combat climate change. But a change in tune took center stage when Trump became the president. Proponents of the withdrawal termed it as an act that was in line with Trump's policy of "America First." The decision to withdraw from the Paris Agreement is a setback in the efforts made by his predecessor to fight climate change.

The US withdrawal from this agreement has attracted criticism from various national and international leaders including politicians, academics, and business leaders. A study by Yale Program on Climate Change

Communication revealed that 7 out of 10 Americans are not happy with Trump's decision to withdrawing from the Paris Agreement. On his side, Trump argued that the agreement was against US sovereignty and would cause many Americans to lose their jobs. It is questionable why it is only the US that can suffer from an agreement signed by 197 nations worldwide. Trump's announcement to withdraw from the Paris Agreement was not conceived well by the state governments. Shortly after making the announcement, the state government of New York, Washington, and California instituted a United States Climate Alliance that would continue advancing the Paris Agreement objectives. A majority of Republican and Democratic Party governors have pledged to abide by Paris Agreement terming Trump's withdrawal as retrogressive and dangerous for America's prosperity. His predecessor's Clean Power Plan was an effective approach to mitigate climate change since it was a strategy that would limit the amount of carbon emission from coal and gas-powered plants. Trump instead replaced this with the Affordable Clean Energy rule that has less strong regulations and does not emphasize on efforts to mitigate climate change. Under his leadership, he has not only halted but also reversed the milestones made by his predecessor in fighting climate change. Trump's rollback such as limiting fuel economic standards of care are more damaging and pulls back the effort to fight climate change. His regulatory rollbacks and his anti-science stance on climate change are not any better for the future of America and American reputation in the eyes of its global allies and the global community at large. Trump's argument that the fight against climate change would have a negative effect on the US economy is far-fetched and does not have the support of economic analysts. It is, therefore, questionable whether Trump has the interest of the future of America at heart.

7.4.Weakening fuel economy standards

Trump's plan to slash the efficiency of fuel standards as well as stripping California off its authority to regulate tailpipe greenhouse emission has received fierce criticism. This plan by Trump's administration has attracted the attention of several environmental organizations and more than 20 states that have moved to the court to challenge the administration's action. The argument put forth by Trump's administration is that the proposal was for the benefit of Americans since it would lower costs and save lives. His administration argues that the proposal would encourage Americans to replace their older vehicles that are not environmental friendly with new models. However, this argument in the eyes of environmentalists is ill-advised because it would lead to an increase in air pollution. Although the plan by Trump administration amount to a less-aggressive rollback, consumer advocates and environmental activists such as Zangee Artis and his peers Jamie Margolin, Nadia Nazar, and Madelaine Tew who founded Zero Hour   Movement have warned that it is a decision that would still have consequences. It is reported that the rollback by the Trump administration would lead to the production of additional millions of tons of carbon pollution into the atmosphere. A statement from the Natural Resources Defense Council also indicated that Trump's rollback plan is unfortunate and disastrous for the global climate. A spokesperson for the California Air Resources Board, Stanley Young said that a rule set by the federal government to cut emissions by 1.5% annually is not enough for the country to meet its goal of improving air quality and addressing the issue of climate change. He further argued that the Trump administration's proposal would compromise the nation's ability to meet federal air quality standards. Apart from having a negative impact on the fight against climate change, Stanley warned that the proposal would directly impact public health.

President Obama's administration posed restriction on tailpipe emissions of carbon dioxide from light-duty vehicles. Trump, however, came up with new rules that weaken fuel economic standards. Whereas this may be a good move economically, the effect of such weakening is detrimental according to environmentalists. In 2019, climate activists such as Haven Coleman and Isra Hirsi cried foul about Trump administration's way of dealing with the fight against climate change. The weakening of fuel economic standards is one of the proposals that Trump brought up but it is not in line with efforts made by President Obama to fight against climate change. Environmentalists have cast doubt on the Trump administration's commitment to the issue of climate change. As things stand right now following the weakening of fuel economic standards, the US stands to increase the amount of greenhouse gas emission into the atmosphere. This contradicts Trump's statement on clean-clean water. With wavering positing on the fight against climate change, Trump's presidency is arguably bad for the globe's climate.

7.5. Lower restrictions on methane emissions

In 2019, President Trump administration's came up with a plan to weaken regulations on methane emission. This move drew the attention of environmentalists such as Vic Barrett arguing that the rule was retrogressive and would harm the environment by exacerbating global warming. This rule was more of an effort by Trump to fight regulations that were put in place by Obama on the emission of greenhouse gases. The standards set by President Obama mandated those in oil and gas business to take responsibility for curbing greenhouse gas emissions. The new rules by Trump are there to loosen the restrictions on oil and gas sites. It is a rule that would make oil and gas companies take less concern about methane leakages from storage facilities and pipelines. Methane is the second most substantial greenhouse gas after carbon dioxide but it traps heat 80 times more than carbon dioxide. It accounts for about 10% of the total greenhouse gas emission in the country. The decision by Trump administration to lower restrictions on methane emission was swiftly denounced by environmentalists and environmental activists as well as other organizations that are concerned about climate change. The general public was not left behind. In a statement from the Center for Biological Diversity's Climate Law Institute by Kassie Siegel, Trump's rollback is reckless and is like pouring fuel on the flame. The Attorney General of California, Xavier Becerra while reacting to this move by Trump administration said that this was one of the most senseless decisions by Trump and vowed to fight it to the end. When this proposal was made by EPA, the NRDC's Doniger termed it as reckless and sinister and promised to see Trump's administration in court if it would move ahead with it. The gas and oil industry in the US has ever remained uncomfortable with methane regulations. Lowering restrictions on regulation was a sigh of relief to them. However, there has been rising concern from the public and environmental activists about the detrimental effects of this deregulation on climate change.

Generally, the effect of methane on climate change is significant and it is questionable how a president of the global superpower cannot see the sense in regulating its emission. By lowering regulations on methane emission, it is evident that Trump administration is putting the interest of the industry ahead of the interest of people and public health in general. Even a layman can preempt the effect of methane on climate change. It is undoubted that the rollback on regulating methane emission is the recipe for exacerbation of the climate crisis that is getting out of hand slowly. It is unfortunate that Trump is thwarting the global effort to fight against climate change. When other nations push ahead on this issue, Trump is busy pulling them back; and with his global influence as the superpower, he might win but what does that win mean for the global community?

Definitely, the world post-Trump presidency might be a darker world. It is quite unfortunate that Trump is coming up with such measures when it is during his reign that methane emission reached 200 million tons. Although the oil and gas industry has advertised its voluntary efforts to curb methane pollution, methane emission still tops the list of greenhouse gases emitted. Methane remains the potential driver of near-term warming. Scientists have warned that the effect of methane on climate change is greater than other greenhouse gases. When methane is released through gas and oil production, it is usually accompanied by volatile organic compounds that are neurotoxins and carcinogenic. These compounds are dangerous to human life. It is thus a worrying trend for Trump to weaken regulations on the emission of methane which has been confirmed scientifically to have effects on human health and climate change. If Trump's presidency could extend into the next two decades, it is undoubted that the world would be the most dangerous planet to live in.

Ibrahim Aldasoqi,   978-1-62265-222-8 (online) 978-1-62265-223-5 (paper)

"We don't need another nuclear arms race to proceed a pace and then to encourage other countries... to develop these kinds of capabilities also. This is not what we need"-
Mazie Hirono

Chapter Eight: Trump second-term effect on Renewed Global arms Race

Trump win will also ascertain if the United States will continue on a path that guarantees a different kind of runaway for global change, increased arms race, and an enhanced risk of nuclear accidents and probable atomic war. Unlike previous Presidents, Trump has taken a much more aggressive and stern approach to the global arms race. He has forged an attack against America's Alliances and withdrew from arms-control treaties.

8.1. The return of the nuclear arms race

Just to give a brief history, the INF Treaty was signed in 1987. It was a treaty between the United States and the Union of Soviet Socialists Republic. The treaty banned both the US and Russia land-based ballistic, cruise, and missile launchers with short, intermediate, and long ranges; excluding air-to-sea launched missiles. By May 1991, both countries had removed 2,692 missiles. They had also carried out ten years on-site verification assessments which ended in 2001. After this, compliance with the treaty was only carried out through satellites. In 2007, Vladimir Putin, during the Munich Security Conference, stated that there was a need to revisit the agreement because it only applied to Russia and America. Similarly, Yuri Baluyevsky, Russia's Chief of General Staff of the Armed Forces stated that Kremlin was making plans to withdraw from the treaty because nations like China were not bound by it.

According to the U.S., Russia had already gone against the agreement by testing the SSC-cruise missile. In their defence, Russia argued that the SSC-8 rocket did not go against the treaty because its maximum range was 480

98

km. There were further reports in 2013 that Russia had further gone ahead to test two missiles in a way that undermined the treaty. In 2014, the United States representatives informed NATO on violation of the agreement by Russia. They repeated the same in 2017 and 2018 where NATO supported America's accusations. Putin denied and argued that it was U.S. attempt to leave the treaty. Dan Bluemental, while working for the American Theodore Postol stated that Putin's main concern was not the treaty but the fact that China was not part of it. According to Russian officials, the United States decision to launch its missile defence system in Europe was a breach of the agreement. Moreover, the Russian experts also argued that America's use of target missiles and unmanned aerial vehicles (MQ-9 and MQ-4) was a breach of the treaty; US officials rejected this claim.

Trump's initiative to withdraw from the treaty began in 2018 when they declared their intention. During his campaign rallies, Trump mentioned that he was considering pulling out from the deal because of Russia's violations. His statements prompted Putin to point out that Russia, before launching the missile, will first eradicate the threat. The other reason for the withdrawal was to deal with the Chinese arms build-up in the Pacific and South China Sea. Kelly Magsamen, one of the U.S officials during President's Obama's reign, said that China's capability to function outside the INF treaty prompted policy maker's way before Trump. The Politico article discovered different responses by U.S. officials some of them arguing that the U.S. had to find a way of including China or employing its technological prowess to develop new weapons to counter the threat. Jim Mattis, one of the US officials, also noted that China was putting up lots of missiles because they were not part of the treaty. Making them part of the INF Treaty or making a new treaty was complicated because of the relation between China, India, and Pakistan.

The Chinese Foreign Ministry noted that the US withdrawal from the treaty would have a detrimental effect. Therefore, the US should think and rethink before making the decision. While speaking on the Echo of Moscow, the US National Security Advisor, questioned Chinese sentiments; wanting Washington to stay in the treaty while they were not part of it. Approximately 90% of China's arsenal would not have been allowed if they had been part of the agreement.

To salvage the treaty, Russia and the U.S. held a Summit in which they failed to come to an understanding. As a result, America suspended its compliance with the agreement on 30th January 2019. Additionally, they gave a six- month ultimatum for Russia to comply fully. Failure to do so would lead to a full withdrawal. In response to the United States, Putin also announced their suspension of the treaty.

United States actions received and will continue to get different reactions. Several nuclear experts stated that Trump's decision to withdraw would have a detrimental effect, and President Trump should reconsider. Mikhail Gorbachev said that Trump's decision was not wise and would only lead to a new arms race. Stoltenberg recommended that NATO should intervene to bring back Russia and also expand the INF treaty to include nations like China and India. Like experts, American law also had contrasting opinions. Jim Inhofe and Jim supported the federal government decision to withdraw from the treaty. President Petro Poroshenko said that the U.S was now ready to build high-precision missiles allowing them not to repeat past mistakes. Trump's withdrawal from the INF treaty has made the world a dangerous place. It has only introduced and heightened the return of the arms race, as clearly illustrated in this chapter.

Besides withdrawing from the INF treaty, Trump also pulled out of the Iran nuclear agreement. By doing so, President Trump has destroyed the United States reputation as an ally and negotiating partner. This has been made worse by his failure to get a deal from North Korea leaving Kim Jong Un unchecked and with augmented international standing. As a result, numerous world leaders are hoping that Trump will not clinch the presidency in 2020 because winning will worsen the situation and make the world a dangerous place. His re-election may prompt other nations to pursue nuclear weapons, particularly countries that have depended on United States security assurance, for instance, those in the Middle East.

At stake are the international non-proliferation governments that America and other nations have maintained in the last many years to convince to stay clear of acquiring nuclear weapons. That the US has extensively succeeded in convincing these nations has been a combination of U.S. bilateral and alliance-based defense commitments. It has also been as a result of consequences, incentives, and pledges made by both America and Russia.

8.2. Trump giving up arms control agreements

President Trump has renewed the nuclear arms race by withdrawing the U.S. from the INF treaty. His emphasis and focus on defending America is leading to the militarization of the US society, be it at the Mexican border or different streets in America. In one of his statements in October 2019, Trump stated that America was more prosperous and was going to build up until both

Russia and China rethink their actions. President Trump seeks to use Ronald Reagan's approach of spending more than the opposition. President Trump is implementing his campaign pledges and overall his military spending is rising at an increasing rate. Figure One: Trump's Military Spending

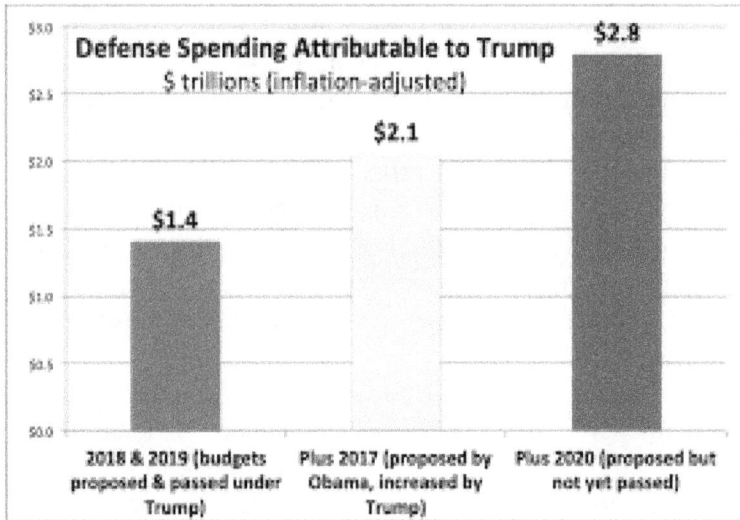

Fig. 8.1: Defense spending in Trump's administration

The graph shows that in 2018-2019, Trump's military budget was $1.4 trillion. In 2017 it was $2.1 trillion, and in 2020, it is likely to reach $2.8 trillion according to the proposed budget.

The inconsistency is that even as threats of nuclear war increases, the cold war system frameworks that assisted in preventing Armageddon is being destroyed; to a great extent by President Trump. In 2019, the United States pulled out of the 1987 Intermediate-range Nuclear Forces with Russia. The United States, through government officials and President Trump, showed signs of non-renewal and a new beginning to a Strategic nuclear weapons treaty which expires in 2021.

The high unregulated contest between the three countries (U.S., China, and Russia) poses more danger. America's plans were unneeded, not sustainable, and unsafe. Given that China has a much smaller arsenal compared to Russia and United States, they are trying to develop nuclear weapons to match the two nations (according to one of the first Chinese weapons research institute). Moscow and Washington's behavior is an excellent incentive despite Trump's call for the disarmament of the three countries.

Like America, China wants its enemies to believe that they can launch their nuclear if need be. The terrible example shown by the U.S and Russia might spread to the likes of Iran. Therefore, by not keeping to their agreements and not adhering to the shared counter-proliferation initiative, the two nations are developing new and dangerous unproved weapons such as the one that irradiated Severodvinsk.

8.3. The possible impact of INF withdrawal

Several analysts point out that the United States withdrawal from the INF Treaty puts it at a disadvantage when dealing with issues from China. This is because China has developed thousands of land-based intermediate-range ballistic and cruise missiles that threaten U.S forces and its friends. The experts argue that this was one of the reasons President Trump opted to walk out of the treaty. On the contrary, some analysts have questioned if the U.S needs to deploy land-based missiles to solve its concerns with China. The analyst noted that America should not just match China's ability because its weapons are not intended to attack China. Moreover, the U.S does not have access to lands in Asia that are within the intermediate-range from China. Instead, it has excellent access to open ocean locations which it can leverage in developing its capacity. Therefore, their deployments should be more of the sea than land. Those experts that support land-based deployments argue that sea and air-based attacks are costly and vulnerable to mobile and land-based missiles.

Analysts further have fears on what might happen to the European security if the United States and NATO ally's perspectives are no longer the same. Once again, we will have to go back to history and review the debates and discussions of the 70s and 80s on the stationing of nuclear warheads in Europe. Some politicians mention that some parties may make an initiative to take advantage of the withdrawal to challenge NATO's nuclear position to foster the political advantage at the detriment of NATO unity.

Europeans greatly value the INF treaty because of its role as the main arms control achievement over the years. For the first time in history, all the classes of missiles were illegal and removed (at least by the two most powerful nations in the world). To the Europeans, the treaty was not only significant for what it offered but its ability to reinforce the idea and sanity of arms control. The INF Treaty for Europe was a way to lower the risk of an increased nuclear use. It was a way to limit the high power competition through an International Treaty and verifiable enactment. Therefore, the Treaty was a vital and practical example of how a rules-based security framework can lower the likelihood of conflict and develops security and transparency through a mutual understanding and responsibility.

Consequently, for the likes of Britain and other European nations, arms control is part and parcel of the political DNA of policymakers and the public. Indeed, several essential voices in the U.S. Congress anticipate NATO to continue its responsibility of offering a balance between nuclear deterrence with arms control.

Trump's decision may also have possible political and military effects. Russia might take advantage of the situation and openly develop and launch intermediate-range missiles. They might continue to blame the United States for its unilateral withdrawal.

On a global scale, military implications are difficult to evaluate. Given that China is significantly advancing in its arsenal build-up, the U.S. will greatly benefit from the withdrawal. Furthermore, the strategy the United States employs, factoring in its allies, might be helpful both militarily and diplomatically. Foreign policy taken by Trump will force or compel China to be part of an arms control negotiation. To be specific, the United States and NATO will have to come up with a post-INF situation that will send a message to China on the importance of joining an arms control agreement or futility.

Furthermore, while launching intermediate-range missiles in Europe could offer some military benefits for NATO, their systems might not be viable compared to air or sea-related weapons which are less costly. There is no sign that America will take such an approach, and any indication might lead to divisive discussion among allies. It is not clear on the level of differences that the missiles will have in balancing forces in Europe.

On the other hand, the Center for Strategic and International Studies argues that America and NATO could make sure that the ultimate credibility of the Alliance's nuclear position, under the scope of United States modernization efforts, will handle modernization of atomic weapons and the delivery frameworks launched in

Europe. It should be stated that independent nuclear forces of Britain and France also contribute to the Union.

Therefore, concerning the dilemma, what should the United States allies do? NATO's statement on December 4th and 5th emphasizing its indivisibility of the Euro-Atlantic Security was the initial step towards asserting its unity and authority. After this statement, the United States and European Allies should begin an extensive procedure to come up with a common approach which should include several concepts. One of them is meeting with NATO Defense Policy and Planning Committee to discuss the effect of New Russian missiles on NATO posterity and feasible conventional options to deal with the issue at hand. Secondly, there should be a discussion between allies on the approach they are going to take to maintain the existing arms reduction agreements or frameworks. The discussion will assist in fostering commonality in the United States and European security; presuming the Kremlin is willing to be a dependable and trustworthy party. Thirdly, there should be long-term interest to work with interested allies to come up with a shared evaluation of capacity requirements to foster stability in Asia.

After engaging the three steps, the Center for Strategic International Studies states that they should be followed up with efforts to disseminate and educate the United States and European citizens on the problems and the measures being considered. Not allowing citizens to have the real picture on nuclear issues facing the world will, in the end, be detrimental to coming up or enacting solutions and hence fostering NATO unity and probably providing entry points for disinformation of any kind. Therefore, Allies must work together to prevent the danger associated with the widening political gap on the

NATO nuclear policy and to show that NATO is keen on promoting unity.

8.4. Eyes on China and Russia

Trump, during his second term, will still focus more on China and Russia because they are the two nations that threaten US hegemony. Analysts and experts argue that the U.S. is currently worried about China while Europe puts its focus on Russia. China and its rising elaborate military sit on top of the United States Defense Secretary list of global insecurity concerns. On the other hand, Europe has a much bigger issue at hand (Russia without the INF Treaty). Russia remains the United States worry, but administration officials want its allies to see China as Washington's greatest adversary. United States Defense Secretary has raised numerous concerns about China's arms race, but it seems NATO's focus is on Russia. Overtime, NATO has focused on Russia. In fact, NATO countries particularly those situated on Russia's eastern flank, have been worried about Moscow since 2014 and the incursion of east Ukraine. The situation has been made worse by Russian President Vladimir Putin who boasts of pioneering development of future weapons questioning the efficiency of America's defenses and bringing about the probability of a new arms race.

On the other hand, European allies are getting worried about President Trump's deals with Russia. Trump's kind words for Putin and his refusal to accept intelligence on Russia's interference of U.S elections and idea to remove troops from regions like Syria where Russia could put its forces. European allies have also been closely following Trump impeachment proceedings that have ended in his acquittal. Additionally, the Trump administration view Europe as slow to react to the threat posed China. America is concerned that China's economic engine is getting more international significance in the military front, international trade, space, and technological progress.

Experts point out that Europe has struggled to handle the Trump administration effectively. Many European ambassadors agree that there are many serious policy disagreements between the Trump administration and European governments. Some of the most notable disputes over tariffs, defense spending, and the unilateral U.S. withdrawals from the Paris climate accords and the nuclear deal with Iran. Other areas that Europe has differed with Trump's administration are sanctions on Cuba and Iran, shifting of U.S. Embassy in Israel to Jerusalem, and approaches on the Middle East peace initiatives.

The immense financial and public attention that Trump has accorded weaponry signifies the priorities that he holds close as president. For Trump, considerations about war, nuclear power and military prowess are important and it is clear that he will do anything to maintain the image of the U.S. as the most powerful military in the world. This is without considering the foes that he makes along the way, such as China and Russia. His priorities clearly highlight the future of America were Trump to be reelected for a second term. A country that is ready for war.

Ibrahim Aldasoqi,   978-1-62265-222-8 (online) 978-1-62265-223-5 (paper)

"Donald Trump has no idea what a deal is. I mean, he's a man who has filed for bankruptcy many times, so he doesn't understand how to make any deals" - Linda Sarsour

Chapter Nine: Trump Misguided foreign policy vision

Despite the calm that has been witnessed in Trump's three years, there is a building crisis in U.S. foreign policy. Trump has been the cause of United States misguided foreign policy. Unlike his predecessors, who valued the importance of having allies, Trump is violating what has taken many years to build. He says that he would only be loyal to those that have fulfilled their obligation to America. Trump just watched as Russia used forced and killed many people in the annexation of Kremlin. Trump is also withdrawing from almost every economic and security agreement, for example, the TPP. Additionally, though China must toe the line, Trump has set up trade restrictions that have affected both U.S. and China's policy.

9.1 TPP Withdrawal

TPP, commonly known as the Trans-Pacific Partnership, was a trade agreement between several nations (the United States, Australia, Brunei, Canada, Chile, New Zealand, and Vietnam, among others). It was signed on 4 February 2016 but was not enacted as anticipated. On January 2017, the elected United States President pulled out America's signature from the agreement meaning that the deal could not come into effect. The remaining nations were left to negotiate another trade agreement known as the Comprehensive and Progressive Agreement for Trans-Pacific Partnership. The new deal integrated a large number of the provisions set in the TPP.

The TPP started as an expansion of the Trans-Pacific Strategic Economic Partnership Agreement consented by several nations, namely Brunei, Chile, New Zealand, and Singapore in 2005. In 2008, more countries became part of the discussion for a more comprehensive agreement; some of these nations are the United States and Japan. In 2017, America withdrew from the negotiating table or deal. The remaining twelve countries decided to continue negotiating. They agreed in January 2018 and in March the same year; these nations signed the revised agreement. However, they changed the name of the partnership to the Comprehensive and Progressive Agreement for Trans-Pacific Partnership. Australia, Canada, and Japan among other nations ratified the agreement in December 2018.

The original Trans-Pacific Partnership Agreement before any amendments had measures that reduced tariff and non-tariff barriers to trade. It also came up with dispute mechanisms that could solve trade issues between member states. The World Bank and the United States Trade Commission noted that the final agreement if sanctioned would have led to a positive effect for all member nations. However, one of the researches carried out by two Tufts University economists discovered that the agreement would have a detrimental impact on the member states. Other observers have pointed out that the trade deal would have been effective in dealing with geopolitical issues, for example, lowering the number of member or nations depending on China trade and raising those trading with the United States.

In 2016, while on his campaign trail, President Trump promised to move out from the Trans-Pacific Partnership if elected. His perspective was that the agreement would interfere or derail the U.S. economy and independence. Trump's strategy was to put America first. He stated that he would negotiate for fair and bilateral deals that would create employment and bring more jobs to America's industries.

In January 2017, President Trump made right his election pledge by signing a memorandum that sought to withdraw the United States from TPP. His action received a lot of criticism both from politicians and technocrats. Senator John McCain pointed out that the decision to withdraw was not wise as it will signal American disengagement from the Asian-Pacific region. On the other hand, the United States Senator, Bernie Sanders, praised the move stating that for many years, America had entered into many agreements that cost its people employment opportunities. Some of these agreements also reduced American employee wages. The graph below shows the stock market reaction on the United States Withdrawal from TPP.

Stock Markets Reaction to U.S. Withdrawal from TPP

● S&P 500   ● Shanghai Composite Index

Source: Bloomberg, One Road Research

ONE ROAD
RESEARCH

Fig. 9.1 Stock Market Reaction after U.S. withdrawal from TPP

Numerous people believe that Trump's decision would profit both America and China. This is because the S&P 500 and the Shanghai Composite Index had the same reaction; they both reacted positively to the withdrawal. The TPP aimed at removing or lowering 18,000 tariffs on the agricultural and manufactured products. It also purposed to boost trade and foster economic growth and ties of the 12 states that had agreed to be part of the agreement. Barrack Obama believed that TPP would have assisted America increase its sphere of influence in the Asia-Pacific countering China's influence in the region.

Experts predicted that the withdrawal would have numerous strategic consequences. Firstly, the withdrawal from the TPP has led to and brought about a number of developments. It has worsened regional doubts about United States global leadership and its responsibility in Asia. There is a significant concern on Trump's government commitment dogged the rebalance because the U.S. was strained by its universal obligation and could only put in limited resources. However, the United States citizens were ambivalent about Asia, given that they elected someone who was opposed to the trade deal. Additionally, Trump's move has further strained the partner's confidence. Sensing this issue, President Trump sent envoys to reassure them of U.S. support.

Asian nations have responded to the United States indecisiveness by reaching out to China to come up with better and beneficial terms. They are also engaging their rivals, mainly Japan, for example, the Philippine President tried to improve its relations with China and increased their ties with Japan. Hanoi, on the other hand, has taken further steps to strengthen their relationships with Beijing while at the same time increasing their pursuit for more markets via mutually-beneficial free trade agreements to lower their dependence on China.

Therefore, the main threat, in this case, is that America might find itself in a passive position as other actors control geopolitical events. The waning of America's leadership position in the world increased the rivalry between China and Japan. Without the United States at the top to mediate between these tensions, the competition between Japan and China could escalate into violence.

Another significant effect of the TPP withdrawal is the unravelling interference of the International order. TPP withdrawal and decline in European advocacy has just added to China's and Russia's intense criticism for longstanding global norms and values. Likewise, China has enhanced and created rival institutions that duplicate then responsibilities of Western-led institutions. The only difference is that illiberal values guide the China-led institutions. Furthermore, when the Trump administration announced its withdrawal from the TPP, China received the news by enhancing their pact in the Regional Comprehensive Economic Partnership.

In an era where there is increased contest on international order, the nation may consent on the need for international laws and rules. However, they disagree on how to define these laws threatening to make international disputes even more intractable and hostile. For example, China advocates for Asian nations to follow the set international rules in coming up with solutions to their maritime issues. Nevertheless, they have reserved the right to ascertain how the regulations are interpreted in Asia. More so, the fall of international support for the

International Tribunal on the law of the South China Sea depicted a fragile International order.

There is also an increasing risk that irritated nations as a result of the impassive Western-led global order, may resort to China, or be tempted to engage in naked assertions of power to guard their interests. Looking at global trends in Europe and other continents, Trump has resorted to increasing his country's military strength and engaging in bilateral negotiations with those against America's interests and also to bolstering the international order.

Notwithstanding, the election of Trump and Brexit shows the increased frustration by the working and middle class due to the empty promises made by economic globalization. Finally, experts argue that even if the United States had agreed to TPP, its legitimacy would have been marred with repeated and lots of issues. Up until regional experts forming these regional trade agreements can show that domestic employees could benefit from the treaties, future America's trade agreements could suffer the same fate.

9.2 U.S.-China Trade War

The China-United States trade war can be described as one of the most significant economic conflicts in the world. The trade war took a more swift turn in 2018 when President Donald Trump set up tariffs and trade barriers on China to change what America perceived as unfair trade practices. Some of the trade practices and its impact were the increasing trade deficit, stealing of intellectual property, and the transfer of U.S. technology to China.

Trump proposed the tariffs to lower the United States trade deficit and foster domestic manufacturing, stating that its trading partners were short-changing the nation.

Therefore, imposing the tariffs was one of the ways of mitigating it. At the same time, many economists and politicians say that America's trade deficit was a problem that could be solved through tariffs.

Currently, experts have noted that the trade wars have made the farmers and manufacturers immense struggle. The consumers have also been on the receiving end because of the high prices. Other than the United States, the withdrawal has also led to adverse economic effects. On the contrary, the other hand, some countries have stepped up to fill the gap.

To mitigate stock instability, both China and the U.S. responded through a tit-for-tat tariff. Their actions have received worldwide criticism from both politicians and experts in the field; for example, the United States businesses have been against the move. The politicians have given a mixed reaction some supporting while others criticizing. Notwithstanding, most of them agree that pressure should be put on China. As of the end of 2019, Joe Biden and Elizabeth Warren had not said that they would remove the tariff when elected. They both agree that the U.S. needed to deal with China's unfair trade policies. Senator Bernie Sanders, on the other hand, stated that he would employ the tariffs as a negotiating tool. However, he criticized Trump for destabilizing the world economy.

9.2.1. Timeline

Below is the timeline of the TPP withdrawal. On January 22, 2018, Trump announced tariffs on solar panels and washing machines. On March the same year, Trump further announced tariffs on steel and aluminum from different countries. The same month, Trump requested the U.S. trade representatives to assess tariff application on

US$50-60 billion worth Chinese goods. Using section 301 of the Trade Act of 1974, he argued that he was responding to China's unfair trade practices, for instance, theft of intellectual traditions. In the same month, Trump's administration listed 1300 categories of Chinese import to be tariffed. Some of these goods were healthcare devices, satellites, and aircraft parts.

In April 2018, China responded by putting tariffs on 128 products from the United States, for example, airplanes, cars, pork, and soya beans which had one of the most enormous tariffs (25%). Other products were fruits and steel piping. Wilbur Ross, the United States commerce secretary, stated that the Chinese tariffs only affected 3% of the GDP.

In May 2018, after much criticism, Vice Premier and Politburo member Liu He visited the U.S. for more trade talks. They agreed to lower America's trade deficient. Treasury Secretary Steven Mnuchin, after the Chinese move, announced they were stopping the trade. White House official, Peter Navarro, stated that there was no trade war but a trade dispute. However, just a month later (after the talks), Trump's administration announced a 25% tariff imposition on industrially significant technology, investment restrictions, and increased export controls on particular Chinese investors. The main objectives of putting up such restrictions were to prevent the investors from importing U.S. technology.

However, in February 2020, both the United States and the Republic of China entered into an Economic and Trade Agreement. The agreement focused on intellectual property rights in the first chapter, technology transfer in the second chapter, food and agricultural products in the third chapter, financial services in the fourth chapter, exchange rate matters and transparency in the fifth chapter, and expanding trade in the sixth chapter, and bilateral evaluation and dispute resolution procedures in chapter seven.

9.3 Tightening the Border

We can expect that in Trump's second term, there will be more executive orders and push for construction of a wall along the Mexican-U.S. border. In January 2017, President Trump issued an executive order on border security and immigration enforcement improvements. The executive order sought to carry many things to secure the United States border. The southern border would be achieved by building a physical wall and having adequate personnel to monitor and prevent illegal immigration and acts of terrorism. Section two of the executive order also demanded the apprehension on suspicion of violating Federal and States, quick determination of their eligibility, and prompt removal of ineligible individuals.

Similarly, in 2017, President Trump issued another Executive Order 13769 (Protecting the Nation from Foreign Terrorist Entry into the United States). The order issued a travel ban on refugees and immigrants from Iran, Iraq, Libya, Somalia, Sudan, Syria, and Yemen for three months. The ban affected nearly 218 million people who were citizens of the mentioned nations. Section five of the Executive Order suspended the U.S. Refugee Admission Program for 120 days. It stipulated that the program could continue for citizens of specific countries if the secretary of state, homeland security, and national intelligence agreed.

Nevertheless, the suspension of Syrian refugees was indefinite. Furthermore, the number of refugees accepted in 2017 was 50,000 lowered from 110,000. More so, when the U.S. Refugee Admissions Program resumed, it prioritized based on religious persecutions. Section seven of the same executive order called for the quick completion and enactment of the biometric entry/exit tracking system for travelers entering the U.S. without determining if they were foreigners or not. Section seven further ordered the Department of Homeland Security to adhere to the recommendations made by the National Commission on Terrorist Attacks upon America (9/11 Commission), to come up and enact the biometric entry/exit system. Therefore, in 2020 we should expect more directives ranging from the Wealth Test and restrictions on travel visas. To further secure the United States border, President Trump introduced a public charge test that gives immigration officials the mandate to decide if an immigrant can enter the United States. By changing the standards of the public charge test, the Trump administration is trying to make it hard for people who are not White to enter into the U.S. Under the new law, immigration officers could see those with an income lower than 250% of the federal poverty levels as a public charge. Therefore, families with an income of less than $64,000 should not apply.

9.4 Withdrawal from Iran Nuclear Agreement

In May 2018, the United States announced its withdrawal from the Joint Comprehensive Plan of Action, commonly known as the Iran nuclear deal. The deal was an agreement regarding the Iran atomic program which was reached on July 2015 by Iran, China, France, Russia, United Kingdom, United States, and Germany. The deal offered that Iran's nuclear activities be reduced in exchange for lowered sanctions. According to the agreement, each three months, the President of the U.S. would certify Iran was following the terms of the agreement. Up to the United States withdrawal, the IAEA stated that its inspectors had proofed that Iran had enacted its nuclear-related commitments.

Trump had hinted during his campaign that he would seek a new deal if he became president. In April 2017, his administration carried an inspection and noted that Iran had complied with the set requirements. In the same year, Trump stated that he would not make the certification given under United States domestic law. He pointed out that the suspension of the sanctions was not appropriate or proportional. Through pressure from John Bolton, Trump withdrew from the JCOPOA in April 2018. He termed the agreement a one-sided deal that should not have been made. He stated that it did not bring calm, peace, nor will it ever do.

Trump's decision was met with varied reactions both from politicians and stakeholders in the U.S and outside. He received support from the Republican Party, the United States ambassador to the UK Nikki Haley, Paul Ryan (Speaker of the House), Secretary of States, National Security Advisor, and Dick Cheney (former vice President). President Trump also received great support from Benjamin Netanyahu, the Israeli Prime Minister. Trump's decision was also supported by different nations like Bahrain, Egypt, Israel, the United States Emirates, and Yemen. However, in the same vigor, he received significant opposition from the Democrats, former President Barrack Obama, John Kerry, among other political analysts like Graham Allison and Stephen Walt. He was also opposed by Iran, the European Union, France, the United Kingdom and Jordan.

9.5.Trump's the Middle East Policy

9.5.1. Trump and foreign relation with Iran

President Trump's relationship with Iran has not been rosy. The relationship between the two nations was made worse by Trump's insistence on revisiting the Iran Deal. In October 2017, Trump announced that he was going to recertify Iran's compliance on the 2015 Joint Comprehensive Plan of Action to Congress. He argued that Iran's behavior violated the foundation of the agreement. He went ahead to request the Congress deliberation on reintroducing the sanctions.

In May 2018, President Trump administration withdrew from the Iran Nuclear Deal. He pulled out from the Joint Comprehensive Plan of Action stating that Iran had not effectively prevented the nation's civilian nuclear program and its aggression. Without giving an example of a violation, Trump issued two sanctions that had been covered by the agreement; aircraft imports and petroleum products exports. In January 2020, Trump ordered the killing of Qasem Soleimani, an Iranian General linked to violent demonstrations at the U.S. embassy. Iran responded by firing missiles on Iraqi bases with U.S. soldiers making the U.S. issue new sanctions. Therefore, the relationship between Iran and the U.S. is cold and might continue to be so if Trump is elected for a second term.

9.5.2.Trump and foreign relation with Israel

Over the years, the United States has been a great supporter of Israel. They have fostered a good relationship while at the same time maintaining a relationship with other Middle East nations. Trump has maintained the same relation and promoted it even more. Immediately after his inauguration, he appointed David Friedman as the new ambassador to Israel. Similarly, Israel's Prime Minister responded to the good faith and announced his intent to reduce restrictions in the building of the West Bank. A few months later, President Trump made public his intention to put up a military base in Israel.

Furthermore, during his campaigns, Trump announced his intention to relocate the United States embassy to Jerusalem and recognize Jerusalem as the capital of Israel. In December 2017, he fulfilled his promise by announcing Jerusalem as the capital of Israel. In May 2018, Trump also opened the U.S Embassy in Jerusalem during Israel's 70th independence celebrations. To further show his significant support for Israel, Trump ratified the U.S, recognition of the Golan Heights as belonging to Israel. Therefore, concerning these events, it is safe to say that Trump, if elected for a second term, will continue his support for Israel.

Moreover, Trump has supported Israel by further coming up with a peace plan. The plan is a proposal to solve the Israeli-Palestinian conflict. The plan which was made public in January 2020, was rejected by the Palestinian government. They pointed out that the plan favored Israel and provided unacceptable solutions.

9.5.3.Trump and foreign relation with Egypt and Turkey

The relationship between the United States and Turkey and Egypt has dwindled under Trump's administration. Also, the relation between Turkey and Egypt has also soared in the past few years. Nations that were ones great allies are now fierce critics of each other. The growing authoritarian rule in both nations has made it difficult for them to engage. At the start of his presidency, Trump enjoyed cordial a relation with Turkish President Recep Erdogan. Despite Turkey buying arms from Russia and using it to attack Syria did not affect their relations. Trump first met with the Turkish President in a NATO meeting in 2018. The Turkish leader praised Trump for not giving in to democratic niceties like other leaders.

While Trump did not in any way oppose to Erdoğan's authoritarian rule, he took a side when it involved safeguarding his domestic political interests. A good example is the release of Andrew Brunson. Andrew Brunson was of great interest to the Trump administration because he was first an American and secondly evangelical. As agreed with the Turkish President, Trump had expected that Andrew Brunson would be released July 2018. However, Turkey did not uphold their part of the bargain. Therefore, when the Turkish government failed, Trump administration imposed sanctions and doubled tariffs on Steel and Aluminum that came from Turkey. Trump administration had expected that when they did so, Brunson would be released. However, Erdoğan remained adamant.

9.5.4.Trump and foreign relation with Syria, Iraq, and the Islamic State

Just like many Middle East nations, U.S. relation to Syria, Iraq, and the Islamic state has been shaky. While on his presidential campaign, Trump stated that the U.S. should siphon oil from Iraq as payment or spoils of War. Taking the oil would actually require the U.S. to go to war with Iraq. Trump's sentiments were regarded as irresponsible and against the Geneva Conventions. Trump supported his argument by pointing out that they would recoup the cost of America's military aid to Iraq and shield its oil infrastructure from being taken over by ISIL. Trump had in several occasions talked this over with Iraqi Prime Minister. Severally, he was advised by his National

Security Advisor that such things are not talked in public because it destroys American reputation and scared people. In 2017, Trump through an executive order banned all Iraq citizens from entering the United States. This was received by a lot of criticism and public demonstrations. It also received numerous lawsuits that prompted President Trump to lower his restrictions and later remove Iraq from the list of non-entry nations.

Trump's antagonism with the Turkish President has come at a really bad time when Turkey is required to play a critical role in U.S. airstrike on Syria. Trump's administration not been able to come up with a notable strategy on the Syrian Civil War. In 2018, former Secretary of State's Tilerson formulated a plan that involved putting troops in Syria with the objective of countering Iran and removing President Bashar from power. Four months later, Trump ordered the withdrawal of U.S. troops from Southern Syria. He requested nations like Saudi Arabia to bear the cost of building up liberated regions of the Islamic State. Moreover, Trump plan depended heavily on Russia persuading the Tehran to move out of the region.

Recently, Trump's administration, through James Jeffrey (representative of Syria) said that it was not going to pull out its troops. He stated that U.S. troops would remain as long as it is necessary. Instead, they were going to find alternatives for fostering Syrian stability and removing Assad's from power. Trump has warned that there will be grave consequences if Assad uses chemical weapons or Russia ends up killing many civilians.

Just like Obama, Trump seeks to bring stability to Syria and the Islamic State without deploying a massive number of U.S. troops. He is taking the same strategy of defeating the Islamic States and pushing other countries to assist the United States attain its objectives. Nonetheless, Trump has not achieved much. The small number of United States troops will not make the intended outcome. Given that Russia, Iran, and Turkey are not will to cooperate, Trump will have to focus more on Iraq, given that he has more influence.

9.5.5.Presence of U.S. military troops in the Middle East and Syria

Even after promising that he will reduce the number of U.S. troops in the Middle East, Trump has not managed to do so effectively. Therefore, for many years now, the United States has maintained a heavy and costly presence in the Middle East. According to recent statistics, the United States has over 60,000 troops in the Middle East. They are planning to deploy additional 750 troops to the U.S. Embassy in Baghdad in response to Iran's promise of revenge after the killing of Iran's Gen. Qasem Soleimani and Iraqi militia commander Abu Mahdi al-Muhandis. In Afghanistan, the United States has approximately 14,000 troops and an additional 8000 NATO soldiers. In Bahrain, the U.S. has nearly 7000 troops most of whom are in the Navy. In Iraq, the United States has deployed approximately 5,200 troops whose main objective is to assist in curbing ISIS. The numbers are likely to decline given that U.S. troops are no longer welcomed.

Besides Iraq, Bahrain, and Iran, the U.S., also has troops in Jordan, Kuwait, Qatar, Saudi Arabia, Turkey, Syria, and United Arab Emirates. In Jordan and Kuwait, the U.S has 2,795 and more than 13,000 troops respectively. In Oman and Qatar, the U.S. has 1980 and over 13,000 troops to aid in curbing ISIS and regional terrorism respectively. Trump announced an additional 3000 troops to be sent to Saudi Arabia to protect it against

Iran and proxy forces retaliation. Moreover, the number of troops in Syria cannot be made public by the U.S. Central Command because of safety reasons. However, the DOD spokesman stated that nearly 2000 U.S. service members were removed after a directive from President Trump. Approximately, 800 troops remain in the region to guard the oil resources. Additionally, the number of troops in Turkey is not clear. Lastly, the number of troops in United Arabs Emirates is 5000.

9.6. Impact of the U.S.-Korea Free Trade Agreement

Even after visiting South Korea, in 2019, the trade relationship between the United States and South Korea still remained shaky; Trump was still considering withdrawing the Korea-U.S. Free Trade Agreement (KORUS), even though South Korea has continued being the US most reliable ally in the Korean Peninsula. Trump's action was received with a lot of criticism with some members of the congress and business community citing it as a wrong move. They pointed out that having strong business ties with South Korea was necessary for the United States economy and the stability of the Korean Peninsula. As a result, in October 2019, trade representatives from both the U.S. and South Korea met and came up with ways to can solve the existing business problems mentioned by the Trump administration. Below are some of the facts associated with the U.S.-Korea Free Trade Agreement.

The U.S.-Korea Free Trade Agreement played a significant role in U.S.-Korean trade relationship. It reduced tariffs for a large number of goods traded between the two nations. Because of the agreement, the United States, for over five years has been able to access the

Korean service market effectively. Korea, on the other hand, received intellectual property protections. The treaty was first discussed and signed by the Bush administration amidst considerable criticism from the Democrats. However, because of the increasing tensions between the two nations, the agreement was given priority by President Obama after a number of changes.

Since taking effect in 2012, the agreement has since received a lot of criticism. The first is that it has increased the trade deficit. They point out that the trade deficits in goods with South-Korea, has greatly increased since enactment of the treaty. It rose from $13 billion in 2011 to $27.6 billion in 2016. While this is so, the figure does not consider the fact that U.S. services to the nation increased greatly and by 2016 it had increased by 26%. Moreover, while South Korea is one of the main United States trading partners, it only makes a small percentage of U.S. trade. However, the US contributes greatly to South Korea bilateral goods. South Korea considers the United States its second most important market.

Putting this into consideration, one may not see (including the Trump administration), the need for having the agreement or trading with South Korea. However, the bilateral trade deficit is a poor method of considering the importance of the trade relationship between the U.S. and Korea. Experts argue that it difficult to identify the cause of the constant increase in the account imbalance given that South Korea has a huge account surplus worldwide. The U.S. trade balance with South Korea has further shown that the Korean economy is growing at a good rate showing Korean demand for U.S. goods has been dropping every year.

Notwithstanding, the most important question to ask in this case is what would be the situation if the United States had not entered into a trading agreement with Korea. What would have happened with the trade balance if this would not have happened? The Independent United States International Trade Commission, employing economic models, cited that the trade deficit would have been more massive. They reported that the debt would have increased by $16 billion. Therefore, the trade balance would have been worse if KORUS would not have given preferential treatment to U.S. exports. Thus, the agreement lowered South Korea's bilateral in goods trade with America by nearly a third of the entire trade surplus. The Independent United States International Trade Commission further discovered that America's trade balance with South Korea was as a result of the augmented U.S. trade balance with other nations. While it has a notable trade balance with South Korea, the U.S. trade balance with other parts of the world is much worse.

Therefore, KORUS has led to United States importers purchasing more from South Korea with minimal net-effect on the entire United States trade deficit but a significant impact on United States bilateral deficit with South Korea; a concept known as trade diversion. Trade diversion usually happens when nations that have entered into a trade agreement buy more from each other than the rest of the world. This, however, does not mean that there will be a rise in import competition for the U.S. industry or job market. Instead, it shows that United States importers have found South Korean goods cheaper compared to those from other nations. As a result, most of them find it proper to buy their products from South Korea. This trade diversion has worsened the trade balance between the two countries.

These figures can water down the benefits reduction of tariffs has brought to both the U.S. and Korea. The U.S. Department of Commerce noted that the States exports to South Korea had created or supported nearly 360,000 jobs. This figure has since increased, and by 2019 it was pointed out that a large number of the exporting firms paid their workers well. Therefore, it is imperative to note that businesses dealing with beef, fresh cheese, and distilled spirits had grown since KORUS took effect. Other industries that have greatly benefited from the agreement are machinery, intellectual property, and business management services. United States Trade representatives' estimated that in 5 years, the U.S. exports to South Korea grew by nearly 40%. They also noted that the U.S. had begun exporting nearly 1000 new goods to Korea.

Therefore, Trump should not be quick to withdraw from the U.S.-Korea Trade Agreement. It has created businesses for many corporations. KORUS was a great win to many workers involved in producing export goods to South Korea. Though the threat to withdraw was to create or invoke negotiation, the danger of withdrawal is enormous. It is likely to have a negative effect on both the U.S. and Korea.

9.7 The Relationship between the U.S and the World Trade Organization (WTO) and the United Nations (UN)

Just like other central partnerships and ties, President Trump has also undermined United States relations with the World Trade Organization (WTO) and the United Nations (UN). Since taking power, Trump has not hidden his disdain for the WTO. In 2017, he said that the WTO has been good but not to the United States. When implementing tariffs on Japan goods, Trump mentioned that his desire to pull out was because the trade agreement greatly benefited China. While Trump had not taken any steps to withdraw, he ordered the drafting of the United States Fair and Reciprocal Tariff Act. One of the responsibilities of the Act was to remove the most-favored-nation clause, which needed the U.S. to treat all WTO members equally concerning import duties to the products. The law would allow the President to raise tariff rates. Given that he withdrew from TPP, there is an excellent possibility that Trump may make useful his threat in the second Term if elected. Trump has charted into waters that no one thought the United States would.

It is imperative to note that Trump withdrawal from the WTO would have its ramifications. If Trump pulls out of WTO, the U.S. will be freed from its responsibility to employ MFN tariffs on imports from WTO party states. Nevertheless, Trump would not be able to alter the duties until he gives executive orders removing set tariffs. On the other hand, if the U.S. pulled out, other nations would have permission to discriminate against her. Therefore, it would be reasonable to only withdraw from WTO if Trump planned to increase tariff rates on other nations. Secondly, in the event Trump pulls out and increases tariffs on some products or services, it would be met by retaliation from other countries on its exports. The tax would make the U.S. unattractive to companies and investors that want to invest.

Additionally, other countries would not be obligated to put a cap on import duties from the United States. Therefore, the U.S. would end up suffering economically.

For example, in response to Trump's increase steel and aluminum tariff, five trading partners responded swiftly retaliating against over $23 billion export. Consequently, it is possible that a pull out and increase in taxes would be met with a similar response. Some countries will opt for exports from other countries instead of the U.S. Moreover, Trump's decision to withdraw from WTO even without raising tariffs is marred with considerable uncertainty which might be detrimental for investment and trade particularly for US firms and employees.

9.8. The United States Relationship with the North Atlantic Treaty Organization (NATO) treaty

Just before he agreed to the Republican Party nomination, President Trump shocked many by his comment on commitment to NATO and defending NATO allies if need be. Trump stated that he would determine if the NATO ally has been committed to fulfilling its obligations to the United States. Political experts noted that it was the first time a Presidential candidate put conditions on defending its allies. Trump was consistent all through his campaign period, even threatening to withdraw the American forces from Europe and its partners if they did not pay more to be protected by the Americans. In most of his interviews, he talked about forcing his allies to shoulder the high defense costs. He also mentioned that he was going to terminate unfavorable treaties that did not benefit the United States. These comments raised a lot of concern among United States American allies. However, they hit the hardest on NATO allies who were worried on the level of U.S. commitment particularly because of the resurgence of Russia. His support for the Russian President and his aggressive methods on Ukraine and Crimea hardly hit Baltic States and NATO allies. Trump's security policies and surprise election has continued to undermine other countries confidence in the ability of America to act as a world leader particularly at a time like this where there is increasing global uncertainty and instability. His total disregard for precedent and priorities that have brought peace over the years has affected the Atlantic Alliance.

As such, the Senate has taken it upon itself to prevent Trump from withdrawing from NATO. They approved a legislation that would prevent the withdrawal. The Senate foreign relations committee noted for the bipartisan bill that required the President's signature. The main objective of the bill is to fill the gap that exists in the United States constitution regarding NATO withdrawal. The Kaine's bill demands that the president look for advice and consent from the Senate before making the decision to pull out of Nato. Moreover, the President would have to inform the Congress of his intention of withdrawing from NATO. Additionally, the bill stated that no congressionally-mandated money will be used in the withdrawal. The Congressional legal Counsel would also be needed to challenge the president's intention in Court. However, in the event they go to court and lose, U.S. pulling out of NATO would greatly benefit Moscow. A divide between Europe and U.S. will benefit Putin who has been trying to undermine the treaty for some time.

9.9 Impact of Trump's Foreign Policy

This chapter is a highlight of the current relationship of the U.S. with other countries under Trump. Were he not subject to checks from Congress and the Senate, Trump

Ibrahim Aldasoqi,   978-1-62265-222-8 (online) 978-1-62265-223-5 (paper)

would have managed to make foes out of the country's most important partners if the cases of South Korea, WTO, and NATO are anything to go by. Still, the country's relationship with China, Turkey, Egypt, and many countries in the Middle East highlight a president without the foresight to make informed decisions. The U.S. main allies such as Europe continue to question Trump's guidance in siding with Russia and the current state of foreign contentions imply what the future of the U.S relationships will be like if Trump is reelected.

References

Abramson, J. (2018). *Nepotism and corruption: the handmaidens of Trump's presidency.* Retrieved from https://www.theguardian.com/commentisfree/2018/mar/06/nepotism-corruption-handmaiden-trump-presidency

American Civil Liberties Union (ACLU). (2018). The Trump memos: the ACLU constitutional analysis of the public statements and policy proposals of Donald Trump. https://www.aclu.org/sites/default/files/field_document/aclu-trump-memos.pdf

Auerback, M. (2017). Explaining the rise of Donald Trump. *Real World Economics Review, 1*(78), 54-61.

Balkin, J. (2017). Constitutional crisis and constitutional rot. *Maryland Law Review,* 77(247), 147-160

BBC. (2019). INF nuclear treaty: Trump says new pact should include China. *BBC.* Retrieved from https://www.bbc.com/news/world-us-canada-49213892

BDI (2010). "America First" – U.S. Trade Policy under President Donald Trump. Retrieved from: https://english.bdi.eu/article/news/america-first-u-s-trade-policy-under-president-donald-trump/

Benjamin, H. Jacobs, B., & Helmore, E. (2018). *US Imposes sanctions on China, stocking fear of trade war.*

Beene, R. & Dloughy, J. (2019). Trump administration shifts course on weakening auto standards. *Los Angeles Times.*

Bobo, L. D. (2017). Racism in Trump's America: reflections on culture, sociology, and the 2016 US presidential election. *The British Journal of Sociology*, *68*, S85-S104.

Boghosian, J., N. (2020). 7 undeniable climate change facts. *Retrieved from: https://www.edf.org/climate/how-climate-change-plunders-planet/climate-facts*

Boyer, D. (2018). Trump interviews four candidates as Supreme Court fight heats up. *The Washington Times.*

Borger, J. (2019). Senate committee passes bipartisan bill to stop Trump withdrawing from Nato. *The Guardian.* Retrieved from https://www.theguardian.com/world/2019/dec/11/senate-committee-passes-bipartisan-bill-stop-trump-withdrawing-nato

Brown, C.P., & Irwin, D.A. (2018). 18-23 What Might a Trump Withdrawal from the World Trade Organization Mean for US Tariffs? *Policy Brief.* Retrieved from https://www.piie.com/system/files/documents/pb18-23.pdf

Carlise, M. (2019). *The Trump Administration Just Loosened Methane Emissions Rules.* Here's What To Know. Retrieved from: https://time.com/5664449/epa-methane-emissions-rule/

Cavaille, C., Gidron, N., & Hall, P. (2016). *Trumpism as a transatlantic phenomenon.* Retrieved from https://scholar.harvard.edu/files/hall/files/cavailleetal2016_trump.pdf

Center for European Reform. (2019). Trump's foreign policy: two years of living dangerously. *Bulletin Article.* https://www.cer.eu/publications/archive/bulletin-article/2019/trumps-foreign-policy-two-years-living-dangerously

CFR. (2020). *Trump's Foreign Policy Moments 2017–2020.* Retrieved from https://www.cfr.org/timeline/trumps-foreign-policy-moments

CFR.org Editors. (2019). *The Strait of Hormuz: A U.S.-Iran Maritime Flash Point.* Retrieved from https://www.cfr.org/in-brief/strait-hormuz-us-iran-maritime-flash-point?gclid=Cj0KCQjw3qzzBRDnARIsAECmrypQ9Xq8UoAaar8qasqvtFdpzgvDlIPoqLXm7IfafzHksYeIa_y0rbIaAj-HEALw_wcB

Cheung, H. (2020). What does Trump actually believe on climate change? *BBC News,* Washington DC. Retrieved from: https://www.bbc.com/news/world-us-canada-51213003

CNBC News (2019). President Trump ordered US firms to ditch China, but many already have and more are on the way.

Congressional Research Service (2019). U.S.-China Trade and Economic Relations: Overview. Retrieved from: https://fas.org/sgp/crs/row/IF11284.pdf

Cohen, R. (2016). *A man who would not be president.* Retrieved from http://www.nytimes.com/images/2016/11/19/nytfront page/INYT_frontpage_global.20161119.pdf

Cohen, E.A. (2019). *America's Long Goodbye the Real Crisis of the Trump Era.* Retrieved from

https://www.foreignaffairs.com/articles/united-
states/long-term-disaster-trump-foreign-policy

Council on Foreign Relations. (2020). *Media Call: Middle East Peace Plan.* Retrieved from https://www.cfr.org/conference-calls/media-call-middle-east-peace-plan

Collinson, S. (2019). The guardrails are off the Trump presidency. *CNN.*
https://edition.cnn.com/2019/10/18/politics/donald-trump-impeachment-turkey-kurds-g7-mulvaney/index.html

Curran, J. (2018). Americanism, not globalism: President Trump and the American
Mission. *Lowy Institute.* Retrieved from https://www.lowyinstitute.org/sites/default/files/Curran_President%20Trump%20and%20the%20American%20mission_WEB.pdf

Denchak, M. (2018). *Paris Climate Agreement: Everything You Need to Know.* https://www.nrdc.org/stories/paris-climate-agreement-everything-you-need-know

Devega, C. (2019). *Donald Trump's war against democracy: is it already too late to
save America?* Retrieved from https://www.salon.com/2019/10/31/donald-trumps-war-against-democracy-is-it-already-too-late-to-save-america/

Edel, C. (2019). Democracy is fighting for its life. *Foreign Policy.* Retrieved from
https://foreignpolicy.com/2019/09/10/democracy-is-fighting-for-its-life/

Edgecliffe-Johnso, A. (2020). Trump urges Davos to reject environmental 'prophets of doom'. *Financial Times*, January 21, 2020.

Epps, G. (2019). *The Supreme Court is Trump's enforcer: The administration seems to*
> *regard "extraordinary relief from the high court as nothing more than its due"*. Retrieved from https://www.theatlantic.com/ideas/archive/2019/09/the-supreme-court-is-trumps-enforcer/598081/

Feldman., S. & Lavelle, M. (2020). *Donald Trump's Record on Climate Change.* Retrieved from: https://insideclimatenews.org/news/19122019/trump-climate-policy-record-rollback-fossil-energy-history-candidate-profile

FiveThirtyEight. (2020). *How unpopular is Donald Trump?* Retrieved from https://projects.fivethirtyeight.com/trump-approval-ratings/

Franck, T. (2019). *Trump totally unchained: second term could mean more trade wars,*
> *Powell exit, new tax cuts.* Retrieved from https://www.cnbc.com/2019/12/17/trump-reelection-could-see-unchained-president-new-trade-theaters.html

Forbes (2019, Aug 6). *Trump's Economy Is Decelerating.* Retrieved from: https://www.forbes.com/sites/chuckjones/2019/08/06/trumps-economy-is-decelerating/#39cc5f064a8c

Frum, D. (2017). *How to build an autocracy: the preconditions are present in the US*
> *today.* Retrieved from https://www.theatlantic.com/magazine/archive/2017/03/how-to-build-an-autocracy/513872/

Fuchs, C. (2017). Donald Trump: A critical theory-perspective on authoritarian capitalism. tripleC: Communication, Capitalism & Critique. *Open*

Access   Journal   for   a   Global   Sustainable Information Society, 15(1), 1-72.

Ghosh, P. (2019). Hawking says Trump's climate stance could damage Earth. Science and Environment. *BBC News.*

Graham, D. (2019). Trump didn't make the storm, but he is making it worse. *The Atlantic*.https://www.theatlantic.com/ideas/archive/20 19/08/authoritarians-are-filling-vacuum-left-trump/596173/

Goldgeier, J., & Saunders, E. (2018). The unconstrained presidency: checks and balances eroded long before Trump. *Council on Foreign Relations.*

Greshko, M., Parker, L., Clark, B., Stone, H., Borunda A., & Gibbens, S (2019). A running list of how President Trump is changing environmental policy. *National   Geographic.*   Retrieved   from: https://www.nationalgeographic.com/news/2017/0 3/how-trump-is-changing-science-environment/

Hanson, V. (2017). What exactly is Trumpism?   *National Review*. Retrieved from https://www.nationalreview.com/2017/01/trumpism-tradition-populism-american-greatness-strong-military/

Hirsh, M. (2019). *The tyrannical Mr. Trump. Foreign Policy*. Retrieved from: https://foreignpolicy.com/2019/10/02/the-tyrannical-mr-trump-authoritarian-impeachment-constitutional-crisis/

Hofman, M. (2020). Donald Trump and the power of incumbency.   *Fortune.*   Retrieved   from https://fortune.com/2020/01/06/can-trump-win-reelection-who-will-win-2020/

Jackson, B. (2020). *Trump's Numbers January 2020 Update.* Retrieved from https://www.factcheck.org/2020/01/trumps-numbers-january-2020-update/

Kahl, C., & Brands, H. (2017). Trump's grand strategic train wreck. *Foreign Policy.* Retrieved from: https://foreignpolicy.com/2017/01/31/trumps-grand-strategic-train-wreck/

Karabel, Z. (2018). A Cold War Is Coming, and It Isn't China's Fault. *FP News. China Watch*

Karen Y. (2018). *After Credibility; American Foreign Policy in the Trump Era.* Retrieved from https://www.foreignaffairs.com/articles/2017-12-12/after-credibility

Kelly, A. (2016). *McConnell: blocking Supreme Court nomination "about a principle, not a person."* Retrieved from https://www.npr.org/2016/03/16/470664561/mcconnell-blocking-supreme-court-nomination-about-a-principle-not-a-person

Lachmann, R. (2019). Trump: authoritarian, just another neoliberal republican or both? *Sociologia Problemas Praticas, 89*(1), 9-31.

Leiberman, R., Mettler, S., Pepinsky, T., Roberts, K., & Valelly, R. (2019). The Trump presidency and American democracy: a historical and comparative analysis. *Perspectives on Politics, 17*(2), 470-479.

Levitsky, S., & Ziblatt, D. (2016). Is Donald Trump a threat to democracy? *The New*

York Times. Retrieved from https://www.nytimes.com/2016/12/16/opinion/sunday/is-donald-trump-a-threat-to-democracy.html

Levitsky, S. & Ziblatt, D. (2018). There are 3 possible scenarios for what a post-Trump America could look like, according to experts. *The Business Insider.* Retrieved from: https://www.businessinsider.com/america-after-trump-presidency-2018-8?IR=T

Lieberman, R. C., Mettler, S., Pepinsky, T. B., Roberts, K. M., & Valelly, R. (2019). The Trump presidency and American democracy: a historical and comparative analysis. *Perspectives on Politics, 17*(2), 470-479.

Lynch, T. (2017). President Donald Trump: a case study of spectacular power. *The Political Quarterly, 88*(4), 614-621.

MacWilliams, M. (2016). *The Rise of Trump: America;s authoritarian spring.* The Amherst College Press. Massachusetts.

McCarthy, T. (2018). Donald Trump and the erosion of democratic norms in America. *The Guardian.* Retrieved from https://www.theguardian.com/us-news/2018/jun/02/trump-department-of-justice-robert-mueller-crisis

Matz, J., & Tribe, L. (2018). President Trump has no defense under the emoluments clause. *Harvard Law School.*

Millhiser, I. (2019). T*he Trump lawsuit testing the limits of presidential immunity, explained.* Retrieved from https://www.vox.com/2019/11/19/20971255/trump-supreme-court-mazars-presidential-immunity-tax-forms

Micallef, C. (2017). Reflections and comments: Trumpism politics: is it truly
   appealing. *International Journal of Social Sciences, 6*(1).

NASA (n.d). The Effects of Climate Change. Global
   Climate   Change.   Retrieved   from:
   https://climate.nasa.gov/effects/

Neely, B. (2020). *NPR Poll: Majority Of Americans Believe Trump Encourages Election Interference.*
   Retrieved   from:
   https://www.npr.org/2020/01/21/797101409/npr-poll-majority-of-americans-believe-trump-encourages-election-interference

Nelson, M. & Gibson, J. (2016). President Trump, the US Supreme Court and public
   opinion. *Public Opinion Quarterly, 3*(4), 1-5.

Newburger, A. (2019). Critics rail against Trump's methane proposal as an 'unconscionable assault on environment." *Weather and Natural Disaster. CNBC*

Palazzolo, J. (2017). Suit alleges president Trump violated constitution. *The Wall Street Journal*.https://www.law.uci.edu/news/faculty/Chemerinsky%20WSJ%201-23-2017%20Suit%20alleges%20President%20Trump%20violated%20Constitution.pdf

Patel, N. (2020). *Looking ahead to Trump's second term.*
   Retrieved   from
   https://www.realclearpolitics.com/articles/2020/02/14/looking_ahead_to_trumps_second_term_142396.html

Paulson, A. (2018). *Donald Trump and the Prospect for American Democracy: An Unprecedented President in an Age of Polarization.* Lexington Books.

Pethokoukis, J. (2020, Feb). What would Trump do in a second term? *The Week.* Retrieved from https://theweek.com/authors/james-pethokoukis

Pimentel, C. (2019). Colorblind Racism, The Trump Effect, and The Blind Side. *In The Myth of Colorblindness* (pp. 113-139). Palgrave Macmillan, Cham.

Poppe, A. (2018). Democracy promotion under the current US administration. In: Democracy promotion in times of uncertainty: Trends and challenges. *PRIF Report*, 19-23.

Post, C. (2017). The roots of Trumpism. *Journal of Cultural Dynamics, 29*(1-2).

Przeworski, A. (2019). Crises of democracy. Cambridge University Press.

Public Citizen, (2018). Trump-proofing the presidency: a plan for the executive branch ethics reform. Retrieved from https://www.citizen.org/wp-content/uploads/migration/trump_proofing_the_presidency.pdf

Ramadan, J. (2019). The Rise of U.S. Youth Climate Activism. *Harvard Political Review.* Retrieved from: https://harvardpolitics.com/united-states/youth-climate-activism/

Saramo, S. (2017). The meta-violence of Trumpism. *European Journal of American Studies, 12*(2).

Schwartz, J. (2019). Major Climate Change Rules the Trump Administration Is Reversing. *The New York Times*, Aug. 29, 2019.

Semones, E. (2020). *Trump impeachment witness: U.S. still 'vulnerable' after Russian meddling.* Retrieved from https://www.politico.com/news/trump-impeachment

Siegel, N. (2018). Political norms, constitutional conventions and President Donald Trump. *Indiana Law Journal, 93*(1), 177-205.

Smith, W., K. (2019). Trump's Economy Is in Dangerous Territory. New numbers suggest that the president's trade war is weighing down growth. *The Economics.* Retrieved from: https://www.bloomberg.com/opinion/articles/2019-07-26/u-s-gdp-report-has-warning-signs-for-economy-and-trump

Smith, D. (2020, January 26). How is the most unpopular and divisive president on his way to a second term? *The Guardian.* Retrieved from https://www.theguardian.com/us-news/2020/jan/26/donald-trump-2020-election-impeachment-democrats

Sorkin, A. (2018). *Why Donald Trump nominated Brett Kavanaugh to the Supreme Court.* Retrieved from https://www.newyorker.com/news/daily-comment/why-donald-trump-nominated-brett-kavanaugh-to-the-supreme-court

Starr, P. (2019, May). Trump's second term. *The Atlantic.* Retrieved from https://www.theatlantic.com/magazine/archive/2019/05/trump-2020-second-term/585994/

Stewart, E. (2019, Jan 15). Trump has reportedly discussed withdrawing from NATO. That would be great for Russia. *Vox News.* Retrieved from https://www.vox.com/policy-and-politics/2019/1/15/18183759/trump-pull-out-of-nato-nyt-mattis

Sullivan, S., Wagner, J., & Pogrund, G. (2018). *On eve of hearing, Trump stands by*
Kavanaugh as third accuser comes forward. Retrieved   from https://www.chicagotribune.com/nation-world/ct-kavanaugh-confirmation-20180926-story.html

Tarnoff, B. (2016). The triumph of Trumpism: the new politics that is here to stay. *The*
Guardian.   Retrieved   from https://www.theguardian.com/us-news/2016/nov/09/us-election-political-movement-trumpism

The Hill (2018). Survey: A majority of Americans don't believe polls are accurate.

Totenberg, N. (2017). *Senate confirms Gorsuch to Supreme Court.* Retrieved from https://www.npr.org/2017/04/07/522902281/senate-confirms-gorsuch-to-supreme-court

Thompson, J. (2017). Understanding Trumpism: the new president's foreign policy.
SIRIUS, 1(2), 1-6.

Thompson, L. (2019). Why President Trump Will Likely Be Reelected, And What It Means For Global Security. *Forbes.* Retrieved from https://www.forbes.com/sites/lorenthompson/2019/02/26/why-president-trump-will-likely-be-reelected-and-what-it-means-for-global-security/#115f1ccb41cb

Thomson, J. (2018). Trump's Middle East Policy. CSS Analyses in Security *Policy*. PDF

Tomac, J. (2019). Trump's presidency is a train wreck. Let us count the ways. *LA*
Times
.https://www.latimes.com/opinion/story/2019-10-20/trump-failures-outrages

Tubbs, C. (2018). Conditions of democratic erosion: has US democracy reached a
tipping point? *Theses Paper.*

Vaswani, K. (2020). US-China trade deal: Five Things that aren't in it. *BBC Business News*.

Wootliff, R. (2017, Sept. 18). Trump to Netanyahu: 'There is a good chance for peace' with the Palestinians. *The Times of Israel*. Retrieved from https://www.timesofisrael.com/liveblog-september-18-2017/

Zhang, Y. X., Chao, Q. C., Zheng, Q. H., & Huang, L. (2017). The withdrawal of the US from the Paris Agreement and its impact on global climate change governance. *Advances in Climate Change Research, 8*(4), 213-219.

www.ingramcontent.com/pod-product-compliance
Lightning Source LLC
Chambersburg PA
CBHW031435270326
41930CB00007B/717